Naked Faith

Princeton Theological Monograph Series

K. C. Hanson, Charles M. Collier, and D. Christopher Spinks,
Series Editors

Recent volumes in the series:

Bernie A. Van De Walle
*The Heart of the Gospel: A. B. Simpson, the Fourfold Gospel,
and Late Nineteenth-Century Evangelical Theology*

Estrelda Alexander
Philip's Daughters: Women in Pentecostal-Charismatic Leadership

Christian T. Collins Winn
*"Jesus Is Victor!": The Significance of the Blumhardts
for the Theology of Karl Barth*

Philip Ruge-Jones
*Cross in Tensions: Luther's Theology of the Cross
as Theologico-social Critique*

Michael S. Hogue
*The Tangled Bank: Toward an Ecotheological Ethics
of Responsible Participation*

Kevin Twain Lowery
Salvaging Wesley's Agenda: A New Paradigm for Wesleyan Virtue Ethics

Mary Clark Moschella
*Living Devotions: Reflections on Immigration, Identity,
and Religious Imagination*

Naked Faith

The Mystical Theology of Phoebe Palmer

Elaine A. Heath

With a Foreword by William J. Abraham

PICKWICK *Publications* · Eugene, Oregon

NAKED FAITH
The Mystical Theology of Phoebe Palmer

Princeton Theological Monograph Series 108

Pickwick Publications
A Division of Wipf and Stock Publishers
199 W. 8th Ave., Suite 3
Eugene, OR 97401

www.wipfandstock.com

ISBN 13: 978-1-55635-975-0

Cataloging-in-Publication data:

Heath, Elaine A.

    Naked faith : the mystical theology of Phoebe Palmer / Elaine A. Heath.

    xii + 124 p. ; cm. —Includes bibliographical references.

    Princeton Theological Monograph Series 108

    ISBN 13: 978-1-55635-975-0

    1. Palmer, Phoebe, 1807—1874. 2. Mysticism. I. Abraham, William J. II. Title. III. Series.

BX8495.P26 H38 2009

Manufactured in the U.S.A.

Chapter 3, "The Via Negativa," was previously published as "The Via Negativa in the Life and Writing of Phoebe Palmer," Wesleyan Theological Journal 41, no. 2 (2006) 87–111, and has been reprinted here with permission.

For Randy

Contents

Foreword

ELAINE HEATH'S WORK BREAKS EXTRAORDINARY NEW GROUND IN the interpretation of the theology of Phoebe Palmer. My own reading of Palmer until I read Professor Heath's work was that Palmer was an interesting but minor, derivative nineteenth-century theologian who at best had offered a crude oversimplification of the theology of John Wesley and early Methodism. What she has done is show that Palmer re-discovered independently some of the deepest insights of ascetic theology from within the bosom of Methodist theology. This totally alters our reading of Palmer, giving her a truly original place within the development of Methodist theology in the nineteenth century. Moreover, Palmer's oversimplification of Wesley and early Methodist theology (the stress on radical personal commitment, on laying all on the altar) turns out to be a very significant dimension of holiness that Wesley, in the interests of pressing the divine side of entire sanctification, may well have overlooked or downplayed. The first of these discoveries would be an amazing breakthrough; taken with the latter we have an astonishing contribution to historical theology.

More broadly, Professor Heath alters the landscape of scholarship on the Holiness movement as well as more general nineteenth century Methodist theology, and ascetic theology. In the former cases the lesson is obvious: we need to look again at the relation between mysticism, Holiness, and Methodism. In the last case, we now have to reckon with the Methodist and Holiness contribution to ascetic theology and expand it beyond the confines of Eastern Orthodoxy, Roman Catholicism, and the Quakers. There are also bound to be repercussions for the interpretation of Pentecostalism.

The reason for Professor Heath's success in this work is quite simple. Where conventional historians work with standard historical categories, Professor Heath brings to the texts a deep immersion in mystical theology that gives her the powers of perception and the conceptual resources that are vital to seeing Palmer in all her sensitivity and complexity. She also brings feminist perspectives to the task. The upshot is that she outstrips conventional historical work in her historical reconstruction of the theology of Palmer. This is one reason why conventional historians will not know what to do with this work; it shows up the poverty of the standard resources brought to the historical task. Yet in time, her reading will become commonplace, and we will wonder why we were so blind to the obvious truth that she has so skillfully unearthed. This is wonderfully accessible, ground-breaking scholarship on the great mystic of Methodism, Phoebe Palmer.

William J. Abraham
Albert Cook Outler Professor of Wesley Studies
Altshuler University Distinguished Teaching Professor
Southern Methodist University

Acknowledgments

MANY THANKS ARE DUE TO FRIENDS, FAMILY, AND COLLEAGUES FOR their part in companioning me through the research and writing of this book. I am especially grateful to William Thompson-Uberuaga for his insight and encouragement, and his commitment to the primacy of spirituality in the Christian life. James Hanigan, Ann Clifford, and Moni MacIntyre have also been wonderful theological mentors. The support of my family gave me much strength along the way. How I wish that I could thank those wonderful Sunday School teachers and pastors of my childhood, though my time with them was scattered and brief. They were the ones who first instilled in me a desire to know Jesus, and to be a part of God's family. Nearly all of them were theological descendents of Phoebe Palmer. And like Phoebe Palmer the power of their influence lives on. Special thanks are due to my editors at Wipf and Stock, who are not only good editors, but wonderfully hospitable people.

1

Saint Phoebe

Introduction

NOW AND THEN THROUGH THE HISTORY OF THE CHURCH A GREAT light appears, a prophet who calls an erring church back to its missional vocation. These reformers are lovers of God, mystics whose lives are utterly given to the divine vision. Yet as Jesus noted, a prophet is often without honor among her own people. In the case of Phoebe Palmer (1807–1874), honor was lost posthumously, for within a few decades after her death her name all but disappeared. Though Palmer's theology continued to be handed on with varying degrees of fidelity through camp meeting preachers and holiness leaders, the holiness movement splintered into numerous denominations eschewed by mainstream Methodism. As Albert Outler comments, holiness, the "keystone" of Wesleyan doctrine, became "a pebble in the shoe" of Methodists.[1] There is also the fact of Palmer's gender, which undoubtedly helped reduce her to a footnote in the official stories of Methodism. The deepest problem, though, is that Methodism lacked the necessary theological framework with which to honor and interpret its premier mystic, for Methodists have long been averse to mysticism.[2]

---

1. Outler, *Evangelism and Theology*, 118.

2. The reasons for Methodist ambivalence toward mysticism are complex, but much of the difficulty is rooted in resistance to "enthusiasm," a pejorative label used by critics against early Methodists (and other Christians of their era) to discredit their claims to revelatory religious experience. To be called an "enthusiast" was to be labeled a fanatic, one whose religious experiences were actually delusions. Accusations of enthusiasm had political connotations, as well, arising from anti-Puritan polemic. John Wesley was accused of enthusiasm because of his insistence upon the vital role of experience in Christianity. Taves, *Fits, Trances & Visions*, 15–18.

For all these reasons Palmer's sanctification theology was separated from its apophatic spiritual moorings, even as her memory was lost. Throughout most of the twentieth century her name was virtually unknown among Methodists. To this day the Mother of the holiness movement still awaits her place of recognition as a Christian mystic equal to Catherine of Siena, Teresa of Avila, or Thérèse of Lisieux.

The primary goal of this book is to locate Palmer's life and thought within the great Christian mystical traditions, reclaiming her importance within and beyond Methodism. Within this task rests a secondary goal, which is to offer a Wesleyan theological framework for understanding and valuing Christian mysticism, while connecting it with the larger mystical traditions in Catholic, Anglican and Orthodox communions.

While Palmer was a powerful revivalist in her own day, until her status as a mystic is fully recognized, she will not have "come into her own." Palmer, for example, could become the patron saint for contemporary Methodists who are drawn to the new monasticism,[3] and who long for the renewal of the church. Palmerian mystical spirituality is exactly what the mainline church needs today to overcome its torpor. Like Wesley, Luther or Zwingli, Palmer was a firebrand who evangelized a sleeping church. Like John of the Cross and other great apophatic mystics, Palmer's theology emerged from her own experiences of unknowing, darkness and loss.

In this chapter I present a brief overview of Palmer's life and theological contributions, to contextualize the more detailed examination of her mysticism and theology in subsequent chapters. Chapter two describes Christian mysticism, locating Palmer's spirituality within the long history of Christian mysticism. Chapter three focuses on Palmer's apophatic mysticism,[4] the aspect of her theology and spirituality that has been the least understood and most controversial. In chapter four a new reading of Palmer's theology is presented, honoring her mysticism and her authority to speak to a drifting church. Chapter five advances the proposal that Palmer is indeed a mystic for our own day, with several key elements of a Palmerian spirituality that are consistent with the ethos of the new monastic movement. While Palmer was a powerful revivalist in her own day, in many ways she could be the patron saint

3. More will be said about the new monasticism in chapter five, but for now see "Twelve Marks of the New Monasticism" at www.newmonasticism.org.

4. The definition of apophatic mysticism is given in chapter 2.

for contemporary Methodists who are drawn to the new monasticism, and who long for the renewal of the church. Saint Phoebe is precisely the one who can help Methodists envision new forms of Christian community, mission and witness in a postmodern world.

Biography

In order to address the issue of Palmer's mysticism[5] we must begin with her context in nineteenth century America and in the Methodist Church. For comprehensive biographies see Harold Raser's *The Life and Thought of Phoebe Palmer* or Charles White's *The Beauty of Holiness: Phoebe Palmer as Theologian, Feminist, Revivalist and Humanitarian.* For our purposes the following survey should suffice.[6]

The Mother of the holiness movement was a native of Manhattan, New York, the fourth of sixteen children born to devout Methodist parents Dorothea Wade and Henry Worrall. Ten of the sixteen children born to Dorothea and Henry would survive to adulthood. As a young teenager Henry Worrall had come under the influence of John Wesley, whose Methodist society meetings made a profound impact on the fourteen year old. Within a short time the Yorkshire native became a Methodist whose faith remained the center of his life for the rest of his life.[7] Along with his wife Dorothea, Henry took seriously his responsibilities as a Christian parent. Palmer attributes much of her spiritual vitality to her Christian parents.

Typical of well-to-do, pious households of the time, the Worrall family was managed with sober but loving discipline. Family devotions, each of which was an hour long, were held morning and evening with Father presiding over Bible reading and prayer. The Bible,

5. The term "mysticism" and the reason for the use of this word rather than "spiritual experience," "spirituality," etc. is treated in chapter 2. For now suffice to say the term as used in this study has to do with numinous experience, with direct, transformative contact between Phoebe Palmer and God. Mystical experience interpreted through the lens of Scripture and uniquely shaped by her Wesleyan Protestant tradition, forms the locus of Palmer's theology, as well as being the driving force behind her public ministry. To understand her theology aright, then, it is necessary to understand something of her mystical experience. It is particularly important to locate her mystical experience within the great stream of Christian mysticism as a whole.

6. Raser, *Phoebe Palmer*. Also see White, *Beauty of Holiness*. For Palmer's journal entries and personal correspondence, see Wheatley, *Life and Letters*.

7. Wheatley, *Life and Letters*, 14.

especially verses that had been memorized, was the favorite topic of conversation around the dinner table. Children were encouraged at an early age to surrender their lives to Christ and be saved.[8] Thus it was that from her earliest memory Palmer describes herself as having had an acutely sensitive religious conscience and never having willfully disobeyed her parents.[9] With a spirituality somewhat reminiscent of Thérèse of Lisieux, as a young girl Palmer longs for opportunities to offer to Jesus lavish, sacrificial gifts.[10] She wishes she could be "like the Jew bringing his costly offering" and feels frustrated that she cannot.[11] Ever feeling her spiritual deficiencies, Palmer describes herself at age twenty as lacking in faith, courage and resolve. In a journal entry dated November 24, 1827, Palmer confesses that she "shrinks from crosses," avoiding the simple religious duty that lies at hand even though in her heart she would like to be a martyr.[12] In time these longings would lead Palmer to the most significant turning point in her life: her experience of sanctification based on "naked faith in the naked word of God."[13] It was this experience that eventually launched Palmer into ministry and from which some of her key theological themes emerged.

Virtually nothing is recorded as to the kind of formal education Palmer had as a child, but it is clear that as an adult she was well-versed in the works that were standard for persons who were Methodist class leaders: the Bible, commentaries on the Bible by Adam Clarke and others, the works of John Wesley and other key Methodist writers.[14] As we shall see in chapters 2 and 3, the writings of John Fletcher and his wife Mary Bosanquet, as well as those of William Carvasso and Hester Anne

8. Raser, *Phoebe Palmer*, 22–26.

9. Wheatley, *Life and Letters*, 17.

10. St. Thérèse of Lisieux (1873–1897) is known for her childlike faith and simple but heartfelt life of devotion to Jesus. Like Phoebe Palmer, Thérèse experienced profound suffering in her life, which became the crucible in which her faith was formed. Also, like Phoebe, the Carmelite sister longed to be a spectacular martyr but had to be content with small daily acts of self-sacrifice in her community. See Egan, "Thérèse of Lisieux."

11. Wheatley, *Life and Letters*, 19.

12. Ibid., 24.

13. This is a phrase Phoebe came to use frequently to describe the importance of taking God at his word instead of requiring physical proofs in order to believe. Raser, *Phoebe Palmer*, 114.

14. Raser, *Phoebe Palmer*, 29.

Rogers were deeply influential on Palmer. (It could be argued from the number of times Palmer cites Fletcher and from some of her theology, that Fletcher's work was more influential upon her than Wesley's.) Each of these authors expresses elements of classical Christian mysticism as being formative in their own spirituality and theology.[15] Indeed, John Fletcher was known as "the Methodist Mystic."[16]

It is also probable that Palmer read at least some of the 50 volumes of Wesley's *Christian Library*, since Methodist class leaders were encouraged to read these works for their own spiritual formation. Here, too, the influence of at least eight mystical tracts and numerous other works by or about mystics were included in the library and may well have left their mark on the Mother of the holiness movement.[17]

At age 19 Phoebe Worrall married Dr. Walter C. Palmer, a homeopathic physician who received his training at Rutgers University. In a remarkable journal entry dated August 12, 1827, the young woman reflects upon her decision not to date four different suitors who pursued her prior to Walter, since she knew she would not want any of them as a husband. For Palmer it would have been a violation of integrity to give hope to any of the young men when she knew she would not marry them. In her words: "I have regarded it as cruel—in fact, wicked, on the part of a lady, to encourage a manifestation of affection, that she did not intend to reciprocate, and since my earliest approaches to womanhood, I have been very guarded on this point."[18]

The Palmers' marriage was happy and, for the time, remarkably egalitarian, with each of them regarding the other as a soulmate and partner in ministry. During the rise of "the cult of domesticity" following industrialization, it was unusual for a married woman with children to have a career, much less to have her husband's unswerving support as she followed that career. Yet this is precisely what Palmer did, believing that to disregard her call to ministry would be to disobey God and demonstrate a serious lack of trust in both God and her husband.[19] Indeed, when Palmer was contemplating marriage to Walter, she recorded in her

15. The definition of classical Christian mysticism is found in chapter 2.

16. Tuttle, *Mysticism in the Wesleyan Tradition*, 138.

17. Ibid., 133.

18. Wheatley, *Life and Letters*, 22.

19. From Palmer's *Memoirs*, abridged in Oden, *Phoebe Palmer*; Palmer, *Way of Holiness*, 61.

journal that he was exactly the kind of husband she could give herself to, for he was a "kindred spirit" and was designed to be a "helpmeet" for her.[20] Despite the evidence for a rather egalitarian praxis in the Palmer household, it should be noted that Palmer used patriarchal rhetoric when describing husbands as the heads of families, including her own husband. This was evident, for example, in Walter's leadership of family devotions.

Repeating the pattern set out in her family of origin, Walter (with Phoebe's assistance) led family devotions twice a day with prayers sung before and after each meal and much Scripture memorization by the children. Palmer's personal "daily rule" included rising at 4 AM for two hours of "reading the Scriptures and other devotional exercises: half an hour for closet duties at midday . . . if practicable I will get an hour to spend with God at the close of day."[21] She goes on to describe her systematic approach to Bible study, prayer for her Bible students and family, and other aspects of personal spiritual formation. Like Wesley before her, Palmer was a natural for a systematic, disciplined and rigorous devotional practice.

Although Walter and Phoebe had six children, only three survived to adulthood. Alexander, their firstborn, died at nine months and their second son Samuel, died at seven weeks. These losses were a "crushing trial" for Palmer, not only because of the normal grief process but be-

---

20. *Memoirs*, quoted in Oden, *Phoebe Palmer*, 65–69. Palmer's use of the word "helpmeet" for her husband is extraordinary, given the usual patriarchal nuances attached to this word. This is but one of many instances where her exegetical ability shines. Palmer is citing Genesis 2:18 in which God declares that Adam needs a "help meet," (KJV) or a suitable helper (NIV). The Hebrew word for helper in this passage is *ezer*, a word that is never used in the Hebrew Bible to describe a subordinate helper but rather is used primarily to describe God as humanity's helper. Yet the traditional understanding of the term "help meet" has been patriarchal, with the assumption that Adam was the main caretaker in Eden, and Eve his subordinate helper. Sometimes the term "helpmate" is substituted for "help meet" in these patriarchal interpretations. Palmer did not understand the phrase to refer to subordination or she would not have used it to describe Walter, for it is clear in her other references to Walter that she did not view him as a subordinate. Her contextual understanding of *ezer* reflects accurately the meaning of the Hebrew text of Genesis 2:18, even though there is no indication that Palmer could read Hebrew or Greek. Brown, Driver, and Briggs, *New Brown, Driver, Briggs, Gesenius Hebrew and English Lexicon*, 740. For further discussion on patriarchal interpretations of *ezer* and the shift from "help meet" to "helpmate" see Spencer, *Beyond the Curse*, 23–29.

21. Palmer, *Way of Holiness*, 80–81.

cause she saw the deaths as divine chastening for having loved her children too much.[22] Rather than embittering her toward God, the deaths of her first two children caused Palmer to re-think her priorities in life and to consecrate herself more fully to God. Palmer's interpretation of her children's deaths as direct acts of God is disturbing to readers today, but throughout most of Christian history Palmer's explanation would have seemed normal, even commendable. Yet there were other factors at work within Palmer's Wesleyan spiritual formation that led her to interpret her children's deaths as a spiritual discipline.

As Diane Leclerc demonstrates, John Wesley himself set the stage for Palmer's understanding of the idolatrous love of family as the besetting sin of women.[23] In letters of spiritual direction Wesley counseled numerous single women to remain single since marriage and motherhood often prove to be a snare to a woman's spiritual commitments. Marriage, according to Wesley, can easily become a threat to "singleness of heart."[24] Wesley tends to denigrate traditional female roles that are totally focused on home and family because these roles so easily lead to idolatry of the family. Leclerc cites Wesley's callous response to the deaths of his sister Martha's children as one of several examples of Wesley's ambivalence toward marriage and family.[25] Of even greater significance is Wesley's position that the idolatrous love of "creatures" (including spouse and children) is one form of original sin.[26] For Wesley the "root of sin" is more likely to be enmeshment than pride.[27] Wesley's position on these matters was handed on to Palmer through Hester Ann Rogers, among others.

Beyond Palmer's exposure to Wesley's perspective on family life, her own experiences led her to see the utter "absorption" of women in their husbands and children as a form of idolatry, indeed perhaps as *the original sin (root of sin) for women*. Again and again she prayed prayers of relinquishment of her husband and children, fearing that she loved

22. Wheatley, *Life and Letters*, 26.

23. Not only is Leclerc's work siginificant for a greater understanding of Palmer's theology, but it also helps to critique contemporary forms of idolatry of the family among evangelical Christians. See Leclerc, *Singleness of Heart*.

24. Ibid., 68–71, 79.

25. Ibid., 83.

26. Ibid., 89–92.

27. Ibid., 113–15.

them too much.[28] The death of her third child and eldest daughter, Eliza, in a tragic crib fire, became the ultimate springboard for Palmer's entrance into a lifetime of public ministry.[29] Leclerc notes the "mystical transfiguration" of Palmer's maternal grief into mature theological reflection: "Palmer's resolution of (vs. rejection of) her maternal grief, can be seen not as dispassionate, but rather as representing a rather mature understanding of questions of theodicy. And underlying her interpretation of such questions is her definition of sin as relational idolatry."[30] As we shall see in subsequent chapters, the darkness of Eliza's death was one of the key formative experiences in Palmer's mystical spirituality and theology.

In addition to the agonizing loss of three children, Palmer suffered from theological opposition (some of it in print), was seriously ill several times with painful ailments and in later life, with what appears to be Bright's Disease,[31] and she struggled mightily with "intense mental conflicts."[32] These conflicts were a mixture of her own temperament, which she saw as being overly analytical and overly scrupulous, and what she described as wrestling with demonic forces.

Harold Raser observes that three critical events in Palmer's life led her into a public preaching and teaching career that rivaled the most popular preachers of her day and equaled their impact. These events were the deaths of her three children, her prolonged spiritual struggle prior to her experience of sanctification, and her decision with Walter to share a home with Palmer's sister and brother-in-law, Sarah and Thomas Lankford.[33]

Both Palmer and her sister Sarah were members of Nathan Bangs' class meeting in the 1820's. Under Bangs' tutelage the sisters began to seek the second work of grace.[34] It was in the shared home of the Lankfords and Palmers that Palmer experienced a deeper work of the Holy Spirit which she understood to be entire sanctification, and there

---

28. Palmer, *Way of Holiness*, 61.

29. Palmer, *Incidental Illustrations of the Economy of Salvation*, 145–46; Palmer, *Way of Holiness*, 151–52.

30. Leclerc, *Singleness of Heart*, 115.

31. Raser, *Phoebe Palmer*, 59.

32. *Way of Holiness*, 64–66.

33. Raser, *Phoebe Palmer*, 33–34, 76.

34. Smith, "John Wesley's Religion in Thomas Jefferson's America," 39.

that she began her public ministry.[35] Following her experience of entire sanctification (which she refers to in her journal as the "day of days," July 27, 1837),[36] Palmer began to "testify" to others of her experience, urging them to trust God's word just as she had in order to enter into the way of holiness. As Raser notes, Palmer curiously says nothing about her sister Sarah having gone through a similar "unemotional" sanctification experience two years earlier, or Sarah being one who helped lead her into this deeper experience of God. Yet with the two living in the same household and sharing so much of their daily lives it is difficult to conceive of Sarah not playing a key role in Palmer's sanctification.[37] We can only speculate as to why this omission was made in Palmer's memoirs.

The first step into public ministry came with the institution of the Tuesday Meetings for the Promotion of Holiness in 1836, in partnership with her sister, Sarah Lankford. The Tuesday Meetings became a ministry of some fifty years' duration. These informal house meetings included a combination of personal testimonial, "talks" (which would have been called "sermons" if given by men), exposition of biblical texts, and prayer. Attendees were urged to take up the challenge to become "Bible Christians" and surrender themselves utterly to the "way of holiness," meaning to the Lordship of Christ, receiving the cleansing and empowering baptism of the Holy Spirit.[38]

The evolution of Methodist class meetings into the larger and more protracted Tuesday meeting was a natural and easy step for Palmer and

35. Wesleyan distinctives in the doctrine of sanctification and Palmer's development of those distinctives are treated in depth in chapter 4.

36. Wheatley, *Life and Letters*, 36.

37. Raser, *Phoebe Palmer*, 44–48.

38. The phrase "baptism of the Holy Spirit" did not have the Pentecostal associations given to it today. Pentecostal denominations such as the Assemblies of God use the phrase "baptism of the Holy Spirit" rather than "entire sanctification," whereas Wesleyan holiness denominations such as the Church of the Nazarene prefer the phrase "entire sanctification." Pentecostal denominations associate the baptism of the Holy Spirit with the alleged initial evidence of speaking in tongues. Non-Pentecostal denominations generally eschew speaking in tongues, and thus have distanced themselves from the phrase "baptism of the Holy Spirit." Phoebe used the "Pentecostal" phrase increasingly toward the end of her ministry, particularly when emphasizing the cleansing and empowering work of the Holy Spirit to prepare believers to do the work God calls them to do. Charles White argues persuasively for several reasons behind Palmer's shift to the use of Pentecostal language to describe entire sanctification. See White, "Phoebe Palmer and the Development of Pentecostal Pneumatology."

Sarah to take. Class meetings were instituted by John Wesley as a means of providing a small group structure in which Methodist Christians could practice charity and hold one another accountable for spiritual and ethical growth. Classes consisted of no more than 15 members who met weekly. Class meetings were powerful means of "spiritual direction in common" among the early Methodists and were one of the secrets to the explosive growth of Methodism in North America in the nineteenth century. Indeed class meetings were the backbone of American Methodism.[39]

Originally the Tuesday meetings were for women only. These meetings provided women a platform for public speaking and religious leadership that was usually closed to women in more formal church settings of the day.[40] Part of Palmer's "three step altar theology" is that one must publicly testify to having received the Holy Spirit in fullness. Thus women were encouraged to publicly exhort one another in the Tuesday meetings.[41]

Two major events took place in Palmer's life in 1839 that changed the course of Methodist history. Palmer became the first woman in New York City appointed to permanently lead a mixed class meeting.[42] This appointment gave official church sanction to a woman to teach and lead men as well as women. The second major event took place when Thomas Lankford's work as an architect led him and his wife Sarah to relocate 50 miles away, leaving Palmer as the sole leader of the Tuesday meetings. Under Palmer's able leadership the Tuesday meetings were opened to both men and women, where over the next few decades, hundreds experienced conversion and testified to sanctification. As many as 300 people came sometimes for the Tuesday meetings.

By 1840 Palmer was a frequent speaker at camp meetings. She quickly became prominent in her region, eventually traveling across the United States, into Canada and across the Atlantic for a four-year

---

39. For more on the history of class meetings, see Watson, *Early Methodist Class Meeting*.

40. Cunningham-Leclerc, "A Woman's Way of Holiness," 11–13.

41. Though Palmer is today seen by many as a proto-feminist, her apologetic for women in ministry was based on pneumatology more than feminist concerns. She was eager to see every child of God actively serving God to whatever capacity God called him or her.

42. Raser, *Phoebe Palmer*, 50, 99.

preaching tour in England. Walter, too, began to preach at some of these meetings, but Palmer was by far the more powerful of the two, attracting larger audiences, and following a heavier itinerary. While Phoebe traveled, Walter often stayed at home attending to his medical practice and parenting. For the first twenty years of her public ministry Palmer usually traveled alone, an exceptional feat in light of the time in which she lived. Walter supported his wife's ministry financially as well as emotionally, never seeming to bridle "at a role which cast him as something very close to Mister Phoebe Palmer."[43] It is noteworthy that neither of the Palmers would accept honoraria for their speaking ministry, supporting themselves instead from their own means.[44]

In addition to public speaking, Palmer wrote 18 books, many articles, and edited the widely-read periodical *Guide to Holiness* (1864–1874). Her most popular book, *The Way of Holiness*, became a bestseller, undergoing numerous printings and being translated into several foreign languages. It is her spiritual autobiography, written in third person and describing numerous mystical experiences.

Palmer's apologetic for women in ministry, *Promise of the Father*, is a superb and unprecedented exegesis of biblical texts used to support women in ministry. While Palmer never argued for the ordination of women in an official sense, this book persuasively demonstrates the necessity for every daughter of God to use the spiritual gifts God has given, including public speaking gifts, in order to serve God and bless the world. The book is a fine example of her clear, analytical thinking and straightforward writing at its best. More than her other work, this volume exhibits familiarity with and competence in the use of historical-critical exegesis, which was new and more than a little controversial in Palmer's day.[45]

---

43. Ibid., 106–7.

44. C. E. Jones, "Posthumous Pilgrimage of Phoebe Palmer," 210.

45. Paul Basset argues that "persons in the Palmerian stream" following after Phoebe, did not use a truly Wesleyan hermeneutic of Scripture and that they tended to identify with fundamentalist understandings of Scripture. According to Bassett, Palmer's approach to Scripture is rationalistic, with a commitment to a "radical doctrine of *sola scriptura*" (85). He contrasts Palmer, who believed the Bible in order to be a Christian, with Wesley, who believed the Bible because he was a Christian (85). While Bassett's statements about some who followed Palmer are undoubtedly true, Palmer's exegetical abilities in *Promise of the Father* belie the suggestion that Palmer always approached Scripture with a proto-fundamentalist, rationalistic hermeneutic. Bassett, "The Theological Identity of the North American Holiness movement."

Palmer also penned hundreds of letters of spiritual direction. By the time of her death Palmer was credited with having brought "some 25,000 people to saving faith in Christ."[46] In addition to this astonishing contribution to the church, Palmer's impact upon numerous key Protestant leaders of her day led to the formation of several Holiness denominations including the Pilgrim Holiness Church, the Salvation Army and the Church of the Nazarene. Her teaching and writing influenced such notables as John Dempster, founder of Boston and Garret seminaries, the presidents of several universities including Asa Mahan (the first President of Oberlin College), Frances Willard (founder of the Women's Christian Temperance Union), and many Methodist bishops. Among her closest friends were Bishop and Mrs. Leonidas L. Hamline, who testified to having experienced "full salvation" under Palmer's ministry.[47] When Congregational philosopher Thomas Cogswell Upham experienced entire sanctification under Palmer's guidance at the Tuesday meeting (1839), it was the beginning of an increasingly interdenominational ministry for the Mother of the holiness movement.[48]

Palmer was also active in many social justice ministries including being an abolitionist and helping to found Five Points Mission, the first Protestant inner city mission in America. Prison ministry, alcoholic rehabilitation efforts and the care of orphans were among her other hands-on ministries. It was their commitment to serving the poor that led Phoebe and Walter to move their church membership from their comfortable middle-class Allen Street Church to a new church start in an impoverished neighborhood near Five Points Mission.[49]

In light of her staggering achievements it is stunning that within a few decades of her death Phoebe Palmer was virtually unknown, although her theological impact continued to grow. In the 1950's Timothy L. Smith and a few other scholars "rediscovered" Palmer, but not until the 1980's when Charles White and Harold Raser wrote biographies of Palmer did she begin to attract much-deserved scholarly attention. As Oden has noted in the preface to his anthology of Palmer's work (1988), she continues to be omitted from most standard American

46. Tucker and Liefeld, *Daughters of the Church*, 263.
47. Oden, *Selected Writings*, 11.
48. Raser, *Phoebe Palmer*, 53–54.
49. Oden, *Selected Writings*, 12–13.

Church history texts and she was never listed along with Finney, et al, as one of the great revivalist preachers of her day. Along with White and Raser, Thomas Oden has helped reintroduce Palmer to the Church. According to Oden, Palmer is the "missing link" between Methodist and Pentecostal spirituality.[50] Moreover, she is in Oden's eyes one of the greatest women theologians of all time.[51] Yet even Oden has not identified the importance of Palmer as a Christian mystic beyond her own Methodist tradition.

To this remarkable woman's theological distinctives let us now turn our attention. It will readily become apparent why Palmer made such an impact in her day, and why her spirituality is so important today.

As we shall see in Chapter 3, Palmer's creative adaptation of Wesley's theology of sanctification arose directly from her own *via negativa* spiritual experience. After her death Palmer's so-called "altar theology" and its author came to be rigidly interpreted in ways the Mother of the holiness movement may never have intended. It is possible, and indeed it is this author's conviction, that Phoebe Palmer's altar theology deserves a new reading, intentionally ecumenical and unashamedly directed toward rediscovering the mystical spirituality that caused the diminutive young Methodist to become one of the greatest women theologians of all time. For I believe that as we revisit the context of Palmer's experience of God, informed by wider understandings of Christian mystical experience, we can rediscover the deeper meanings of her altar theology, meanings that have been obscured by the "reification of sanctification" that took place among her theological progeny.[52]

Theological Distinctives: Altar Theology and Entire Sanctification

To understand Palmer's altar theology and her creative adaptation of John Wesley's theology of entire sanctification it is necessary briefly to revisit Wesley's experience and doctrine of "perfecting grace," or entire sanctification.

---

50. Ibid., 16–17.

51. Ibid., 14–15.

52. See Truesdale, "Reification of Sanctification."

When John Wesley's "heart was strangely warmed," the pivotal numinous experience of May 24, 1738, it changed the entire course of his ministry. Wesley describes the event as follows:

> In the evening I went very unwillingly to a society in Aldersgate Street, where one was reading Luther's preface to the Epistle to the Romans. About a quarter before nine, while he was describing the change which God works in the heart through faith in Christ, I felt my heart strangely warmed. I felt I did trust in Christ, Christ alone, for salvation: and an assurance was given me, that He had taken away my sins, even mine, and saved me from the law of sin and death.[53]

The experience of having his "heart strangely warmed" with assurance about his salvation, and the subsequent power Wesley experienced to resist temptation and to do the ministry to which God had called him, were key experiences Wesley had that contributed to his theology of sanctification. As was the case with Martin Luther, whose preface to the Epistle to the Romans was the vehicle of Wesley's profound experience, Wesley's faith moved from an intellectual assent and an anxious, works-centered faith to an emotionally experienced faith, one which was marked with new power, new vision and new love, one which had grace as its central theme.

From early childhood Wesley was committed to the Christian faith and was a pious man of strong principle. He had considerable leadership ability. Prior to his Aldersgate experience Wesley had already been involved in spiritual leadership at Oxford, with the formation of the Holy Club. As an ordained Anglican minister John Wesley and his brother Charles had already made a missions trip to Georgia. Thus the Aldersgate experience could not exactly be described as one of conversion to the Christian faith. It was, rather, a deeper work of God, a turning point for the founder of the people called Methodists.

As a result of his own experience and from his study of certain Eastern (and mostly pre-Augustinian) patristic writers, as well as the writings of William Law, Jeremy Taylor and Thomas à Kempis, Wesley came to understand the experience of entire sanctification to be both an event and a process subsequent to conversion, one which would

---

53. Wesley, *John Wesley's Journal*, 51.

culminate in the believer's being "perfected" in divine love and likeness.[54] Wesley did not present a norm for the amount of time or experience that must lapse before a converted person is ready to experience entire sanctification. Instead, Wesley urged new converts to quickly open themselves completely to the "perfecting grace" of sanctification.[55]

Wesley wrote and preached copiously on sanctification as the grace of God which leads to holiness, or teleological completion of love toward God and neighbor. Using the Greek New Testament for his text, Wesley focused on the Greek word *teleiotes* (Col 3:14; Heb 6:1) in which perfection is understood to mean maturation or completion.[56]

For Wesley the sanctified Christian life is to be one of increasing holiness, a life of increasing love of God and neighbor. Sin no longer has inevitable power in the sanctified believer. While temptation is not eradicated, the believer is empowered by the indwelling Holy Spirit to effectively resist temptation. In addition to evident outward fruits of holiness in one's life there should be an "inward witness" or emotional assurance that one is being transformed by God's holy love and that one is indeed "going on to perfection." (Wesley's stress on experiencing an inward witness or assurance comes directly from his own experience at Aldersgate.) To summarize then, in the words of Michael Christensen, for Wesley entire sanctification or Christian perfection is understood:

> . . . as an experience of grace, subsequent to salvation, with the effect that the Holy Spirit takes full possession of the soul, sanctifies the heart, and empowers the will so that one can love God and others blamelessly in this life. One is justified and then sanctified—understood as imparted, not just imputed on the basis of what Christ accomplished on the cross. The power of sin in the believer's life is either eradicated or rendered inoperative as one participates in the higher life of the divine.[57]

Wesley's clearest and most definitive teaching on "the second blessing" of entire sanctification is found in his treatise: *A Plain Account of*

---

54. See Christensen, "Theosis and Sanctification," 71–93.

55. White, "Phoebe Palmer and the Development of Pentecostal Pneumatology," 202.

56. Oden, *John Wesley's Scriptural Christianity*, 320.

57. Christensen, "Theosis and Sanctification," 71. For a more detailed but concise exposition of Wesley's sanctification theology, using many primary sources, see Oden, *John Wesley's Scriptural Christianity*, 311–43.

Christian Perfection. John Fletcher, considered by some to be the great-est early Methodist theologian, developed Wesley's doctrine of Christian perfection in a treatise of his own entitled: *Check to Antinomianism, or A Vindication of the Rev. Mr. Wesley's Minutes*.[58] The book is a series of five letters written to defend Wesley's Arminian position regarding predes-tination, grace and free will.[59] Both Wesley and Fletcher's primary theo-logical concern in the Calvinist controversy was, according to Thomas A. Langford, that "the Calvinist position would result in antinomianism and hence undercut the drive for Christian holiness."[60]

In *Check to Antinomianism*, Fletcher does more than systematize and expound Wesley's teaching on Christian perfection. He goes on to make new contributions, which would later be adapted into Palmer's sanctification theology. These new ideas include Pentecostal language in regard to sanctification, linking the Baptism of the Holy Spirit to entire sanctification; a shifted stress toward the instantaneous event of sanctification over the process of sanctification; and an understanding of human history as having taken place in three dispensations: the dis-pensation of the Father (Old Testament era), the Son (New Testament era), and the Holy Spirit (the Church since Pentecost).[61] Of these three innovations the first two would figure most prominently in the thought of Palmer.

An excerpted version of *First Check to Antinomianism* was later published with a letter (written in 1796) by Thomas Rutherford and entitled *Christian Perfection*. In the shorter work Fletcher defines entire sanctification or Christian perfection with customary poetic elegance:

> In other words, Christian perfection is a spiritual constellation made up of these gracious stars,—perfect repentance, perfect faith, perfect humility, perfect meekness, perfect self-denial, perfect resignation, perfect hope, perfect charity for our visible

---

58. Fletcher had been designated by Wesley to be Wesley's successor, but Fletcher preceded Wesley in death. Fletcher, *Check to Antinomianism*. The extracted treatise is published as: *Christian Perfection: Being an Extract from the Rev. John Fletcher's Treatise on That Subject*.

59. The controversy between Calvinists and Arminians was the most heated debate marking the Second Great Awakening, the series of revivals that spanned the latter years of the eighteenth century and touched Christians from virtually all denomina-tions in the U.S. with a renewed call to salvation and holiness of life.

60. Langford, *Practical Divinity*, 51.

61. Ibid., 53.

enemies, as well as for our earthly relations; and, above all, perfect love for our invisible God, through the explicit knowledge of our Mediator Jesus Christ. And as this last star is always accompanied by all the others, as Jupiter is by his satellites, we frequently use, as St. John, the phrase "perfect love," instead of the word "perfection"; understanding by it the pure love of God, shed abroad in the heart of established believers by the Holy Ghost, which is abundantly given them under the fullness of the Christian dispensation.[62]

By the time Palmer was born, just sixteen years after Wesley's death, revival fire burned hot across New York and the rest of New England. The Second Great Awakening reached from the classrooms of Yale to primitive frontier settlements to genteel parlors of upper class New Yorkers, drawing thousands to a deeper commitment of life and self to Christ.

Revival preachers such as Charles Grandison Finney (1792–1875) used hard-hitting, emotional messages to persuade assembled listeners to repent of all sin and experience full salvation. Unlike the preachers of the First Great Awakening, who were nearly all Calvinistic, these preachers were primarily Arminian.[63] The Gospel was to be preached to all people because the possibility of repentance existed for all. Penitents came forward to the "mourners' bench," a long bench near the pulpit where sins were confessed and forgiveness received.[64] Protracted camp meetings were the new method for revival preachers wanting to reach increasingly large audiences. While some camp meetings such as Cane Ridge, Kentucky, became known for strange physical manifestations (barking, lying prostrate, shaking, and other experiences), in general the revivals led many people to a deeper life of piety. Penitents were instructed to express their newfound faith in a life of holiness, including attention to social justice issues such as abolition, temperance and

---

62. Fletcher, *Christian Perfection*, 9–10.

63. Some of the Second Great Awakening preachers were Arminian despite their Calvinist background, Charles Finney (a Presbyterian) being a prime example.

64. Fitzmier points out Finney's previous career as a lawyer and its influence on his innovations in ministry, such as use of the mourner's bench which is much like the witness stand in a court of law. Finney also frequently appealed to juridical imagery to communicate the Gospel. See Fitzmier, "Second Great Awakening." Legal language and the use of Finney's mourner's bench, etc. become important in the development of Palmer's preaching career, which in every way was equal to that of Finney.

the needs of impoverished immigrants. Thus the call to salvation had widespread social ramifications, leading to the establishment of many social justice ministries.

It was into this climate of revival that Palmer was born. From her earliest memories Palmer describes herself as being a spiritually sensitive child, eager to please God and parents.[65] Ironically, the absence of any period in her life in which she disavowed the faith of her parents, created the angst which eventually led to Palmer's sanctification experience. Her memoirs record:

> So early in life was the love of God shed abroad in her heart, that occasionally it was a subject of perplexity with her, that she could not so distinctly trace the hour of her conversion, as many others. But there was a time in her young child-days, making a turning point in her experience that did not admit of questioning. Seeing a number of persons at the altar of prayer as seekers of salvation, some of whom seemed to be the subjects of exciting influences, such as she had not felt, she went forward and knelt among them. She hoped that by some mysterious power she might also receive like influence, and be led to cry out in the agony of deep conviction. No such feelings were given, but, on the contrary, a realization of trust and hope in God, that she should not be cast off, but that Jesus loved and would save her. The tempter said, "The reason you feel thus, is because you are not convicted. So you may just as well give up the whole matter." "That I will never do. No! Never!" said the young seeker. "I will continue to seek as long as I live, though it may be till I am three-score, or a hundred years old. I will continue to seek, and if I find mercy at last, I will thank the Lord that I ever lived, and praise Him forever!" That moment Jesus revealed Himself as never before to His little one, and she went on her way rejoicing."[66]

Palmer's early childhood conversion experience at the "altar" (the mourner's bench) was to repeat itself, in a sense, in her young adulthood when she would struggle with guilt and shame over her lack of emotion as she sought the "second blessing" of entire sanctification. Under the tutelage of Wesley, revival preachers insisted that the "inner witness" or "assurance" is always present when one is sanctified. There was also an often unspoken assumption that repentance is accompa-

---

65. Wheatley, *Life and Letters*, 17.
66. Ibid., 18–19.

nied by tears and much sorrow. While others wept and groaned at the mourner's bench Palmer knelt, dry-eyed and sober, longing for even a trickle of tears. While others rejoiced with exceeding great joy at the manifest presence of God, Palmer watched and yearned, believing the message but feeling little.

> I have just been spending three or four days at Sing-Sing camp meeting. The Lord manifested himself most graciously to His people. My own soul was refreshed. The Lord has given me a longing desire for purity. I am sure I would not knowingly keep back anything from God. But alas! There must be some hindrance, or I should consciously enjoy the witness that Jesus reigns the Supreme Object of my affections.[67]

In this and other journal entries written prior to her momentous "Day of Days," Palmer lamented the absence of emotion as she sought the deeper experience of God proclaimed by revival preachers. She never questioned the reality of the emotional experience others have, but rather saw her own lack of feeling as a personal deficiency.

On July 27, 1837, the devout seeker finally had a breakthrough. Writing in *Faith and Its Effects,*[68] *The Way of Holiness* and her memoirs, Palmer describes the experience as the pivotal turning point of her journey, the experience "which she regarded as the most eventful of all her religious career."[69] The climax of the "day of days" came after a protracted dialogue between Palmer and the voice of God, which she perceived to be speaking to her directly, through Scripture. The most detailed version of the struggle leading up to Palmer's experience of full surrender involves eight points of temptation.[70] These were understood by Palmer to be direct attacks from Satan to try to prevent her from receiving God's fullest blessing. This series of eight temptations is of great significance in understanding the mysticism of Palmer's sanctification experience and subsequently, her sanctification theology. In some ways the eight temptations and her response to them are typical and representative of her mysticism overall. Since that is the case, the nature of the temptations and Palmer's response to them is treated in subsequent

---

67. Ibid., 28–29.

68. Palmer, *Faith and Its Effects*; Palmer, *Way of Holiness*.

69. Wheatley, *Life and Letters*, 36.

70. Oden, *Selected Writings*, 115.

chapters focusing on mysticism. For now it is sufficient to know that the temptations had to do with what I propose was Palmer's own form of *via negativa* spirituality, or her "not knowing" and her lack of emotions despite her deep faith.

The first step toward entire sanctification came when Palmer resolved to be a "Bible Christian"[71] no matter what the cost would be. With a prayer of surrender like those of many saints before her, Palmer committed everything she was and had to the will of God. For her this meant a covenant to be a "Bible Christian":

> I never made much progress in the career of faith, until I most solemnly resolved, in the strength of the Lord Jehovah, that I would do every duty, though I might die in the effort. From that hour my course was onward and upward. I also covenanted with God that I would be a Bible Christian, and most carefully seek to know the mind of the spirit, as recorded in the written word, though it might lead to an experience unlike all the world beside. I had often prayed for holiness of heart, before, but do not remember now that holiness, as a blessing in *name*, was on my mind; my highest and all-engrossing desire was to be a Bible Christian.[72]

As Palmer worked through the eight temptations, answering each one with Scripture, she realized that she could trust the promises in the Bible whether she emotionally felt anything or not. As she wrestled with the desire for an emotional manifestation that would prove she had been sanctified, Palmer sensed the Holy Spirit challenge her to believe the written word of God as quickly as she would believe an audible voice from heaven, telling her she was sanctified.[73] The written word of God promised: "I will receive you," therefore, Palmer reasoned, it was her duty and gift to believe this promise and begin to live as if it were true instead of waiting for some outward sign.[74] She agreed with God that she would "lay hold of the Word" in this promise and trust that she had been fully received and fully sanctified. Even if she never felt any

---

71. Palmer uses the phrase "Bible Christian" to refer to a Christian who has embraced the "way of holiness" as commanded by God in Scripture. See Palmer, *The Way of Holiness*, 43.

72. Wheatley, *Life and Letters*, 36.

73. Ibid., 40.

74. Ibid., 41.

religious emotion for the rest of her life, she wrote, she resolved to walk by faith and "hold on in the death struggle."[75]

In Palmer's book *Faith and Its Effects* her account of the "day of days" focuses primarily on her struggle to relinquish her husband, Walter, as the object of her supreme affections. (This struggle is one of the eight temptations described in her memoirs.) She had already interpreted her two infant sons' deaths as the judgment of God because of what she felt was her idolatrous love for them. Now she began to feel that her deep love for Walter and the oneness that existed between them could be a hindrance to her loving God first and best.[76] The story of Abraham's sacrifice of Isaac was the biblical metaphor that guided Palmer's prayer as she finally gave Walter to God in surrender:

> I could just as readily have said, "Take *life*" as I could have said, "Take friends"; for that which was just as dear, if not dearer, than life, had been required. And when I said, "Take him who is the supreme object of my earthly affections," I, from that moment felt that I was fully set apart for God, and began to say, "Every tie that has bound me to earth is severed." I could now as easily have doubted of my existence as to have doubted that God was the supreme object of my affections.[77]

Thus the day of days was not one in which Palmer finally had the emotional spiritual experience she longed for, but rather one in which she settled the question of the role of emotion and other signs in regard to trusting God for sanctification. It was a day of purification and release, in a sense, from the need for emotional religious experience. It was also a day of transaction between Palmer and God, in which she believed she had finally, irrevocably placed everything in her life on the altar so that no thing could ever again come before God in her life.

As she subsequently began to articulate her experience of "naked trust in the naked word of God" regarding sanctification, Palmer developed a new "shorter way" for others to use in seeking sanctification.

---

75. Ibid.

76. We cannot help but observe that Palmer was capable of deep and passionate feeling, as expressed toward her husband and children. Perhaps the presence of strong feeling for her family presented too painful a contrast with her seeming absence of emotionalism toward God, contributing to her conviction that her love for her children and Walter were at times idolatrous.

77. Quoted in Oden, *Selected Writings*, 115.

She also articulated what came to be known as her distinctive "altar theology" or "altar covenant," which was foundational to the shorter way. It was not Palmer's desire to create a new theology of sanctification, but rather to help other strugglers trust God's word and begin to act upon it despite their own fluctuating emotions. Palmer believed that she was teaching the same principles that Wesley had taught in regard to sanctification.

The shorter way involves three steps, each of which has its own assumptions about Scripture, faith and the nature of salvation. These steps are entire consecration, faith, and testimony. The warp and woof of the whole process is Palmer's understanding of what holiness is, how it is gained and how it can be lost. For her, holiness is the experience of being entirely devoted to God, of being a living sacrifice on the altar of Christ, of being continuously "washed, cleansed, and renewed after the image of God" as one is ceaselessly presented to God.[78] Using the ancient hermeneutical method of "pearl-stringing" Palmer cites numerous texts from both Old Testament and New Testament in which God's people are commanded to be holy or be sanctified.[79] Of these texts, Hebrews 12:14 is most prominent: "Follow peace with all men, and holiness, without which no man will see the Lord."

At times Palmer goes so far as to give the impression that a professing Christian still may not be ready for heaven and may actually be in danger of hell if he or she has not entered the way of holiness, since "without holiness, no man will see the Lord."[80] The only way to stay holy is to keep everything "on the altar." For in Palmer's altar theology it is the altar that sanctifies the gift. And, true to her Wesleyan, Arminian theological heritage, she believes that the Christian never loses his or her free will, with which continuous decisions are made about keeping on or removing from the altar, that which has previously been consecrated.

As we shall see, the "shorter way" of sanctification is both an event and a process. Though many of her theological progeny have focused on the instantaneous side of the shorter way (having a personal "day of

---

78. Excerpted in Oden, *Selected Writings*, 189. The text is originally from Palmer, *Entire Devotion to God*, section II.

79. Ibid.

80. White, *Beauty of Holiness*, 133–34. Phoebe quotes Heb 12:14, among other texts.

days," so to speak, to which one could point as the day of one's sanctification), it is already clear from the brief citations of her own descriptions of the shorter way that a daily process of surrender is involved, one which requires all three "steps" on an ongoing basis.[81] Palmer issues repeated admonitions against losing one's holiness, and the need to walk faithfully day by day in order to retain a state of sanctification. Despite Palmer's teaching on the ongoing process of being made holy, this side of her teaching was subsequently minimized, while the three-step, shorter way was emphasized as an instantaneous event by those who followed her. The neglect of focus on the process of the shorter way receives more detailed treatment in chapter four, for it is one of the symptoms of Palmer's theology not having been understood sufficiently in light of her mystical experience.

Palmer's "altar theology," the corollary of her shorter way of sanctification, centers on two concepts: first that the altar sanctifies the gift, and second that Christ himself is the altar. As always, these convictions are based upon Scripture. Palmer's understanding that the altar sanctifies the gift is based upon Matthew 23:19, in which Jesus answers his critics with a quote from Exodus 29:37. The gift is not intrinsically holy, rather the altar of sacrifice is what makes the gift holy.

> It is only by an entire and continual reliance on Christ, that a state of entire sanctification can be retained. The sacrifices under the old dispensation were sanctified by the altar upon which they were laid. Had the offerer resumed the sacrifice, to the degree he resumed it, to that degree it would have ceased to be sanctified; for it was the *altar* that sanctified the gift.[82]

Palmer goes on to argue that Christ is not only the sacrifice for sin, but he is also the altar:

> The altar, thus provided by the conjoint testimony of the Father, Son, and Holy Spirit, is Christ. His sacrificial death and sufferings are the sinner's plea; the immutable promises of the Lord Jehovah the ground of claim.[83]

81. For more on the reification of the instantaneous side of the shorter way, see Truesdale, "Reification of Sanctification."

82. Excerpted in Oden, *Selected Writings*, 200. Originally found in *Entire Devotion to God*, section XVI.

83. *Way of Holiness*, 43. This is but one of numerous instances in which this claim is made.

Palmer's understanding of Christ as the altar is based upon a particular interpretation of Heb 13:10 in which believers are assured: "We have an altar from which those who officiate in the tent have no right to eat." Following Adam Clarke, Palmer understands the altar in this passage and the rest of Hebrews to be Christ. In Hebrews Christ is all three: the sacrifice, the priest and the altar. This interpretation is consistent not only with Clarke, but also with much of Church tradition since antiquity.[84]

Understanding, then, the foundation of her altar theology, let us consider the three parts of the shorter way of sanctification. The first step of the shorter way is the step of entire consecration, in which the individual takes inventory of every part of his or her life, willfully and with irrevocable commitment placing everything on the "altar" which is Christ himself. Nothing is held back. Romans 12:1–2, in which Paul exhorts believers to present themselves as living sacrifices is the scriptural command for this step. As part of this step the believer also implores God to reveal if there is anything that has not been surrendered. If anything is held back, whether it is a relationship, possessions, or even the sin of doubt, one cannot expect to receive the full blessing of sanctification.[85]

For Palmer, this inventory and prayer has the nature of a legal document such as a last will and testament. In her book *Entire Devotion to God* Palmer includes a sample covenant prayer that can be personalized.[86] More will be said about this covenant prayer in subsequent chapters on mysticism.

The second step of the shorter way is the exercise of faith: willfully trusting the promise of God in Scripture concerning sanctification, regardless of outward signs, emotions, or religious manifestations.[87]

84. Raser, *Phoebe Palmer*, 160. Observe that contemporary NT scholars including Attridge and Lane are in agreement with Palmer's exegesis of the altar in Hebrews. See Attridge, *Epistle to the Hebrews*, 391. Also see Lane, *Hebrews 9–13*, vol. 48, 538–39. "Altar" in Heb 13:10 is a metonymy for sacrifice, according to Lane, with Christ being the perfect and final sacrifice.

85. White, *Beauty of Holiness*, 136–37.

86. Ibid., 247.

87. It is important to note, however, that Palmer expected a holy lifestyle ultimately to manifest itself in those who claim to be sanctified. She minces no words in warning that Christians whose lives do not reflect the indwelling Christ will be held directly accountable by God. Palmer blames hypocritical Christians for giving faith a bad name

This step requires "naked faith in the naked word of God." Since God promises to receive all who fully consecrate themselves to him (2 Cor 6:16—7:1), the believer has no reason to fear being rejected by God. Even if the one seeking holiness is not sure about having confessed all sin and consecrated everything to God, there is no reason to doubt because Phil 3:15 promises that if the Christian thinks incorrectly about something but is still open to God, God will surely reveal and correct the incorrect thinking.[88]

To doubt that one is sanctified after having fully consecrated oneself is to doubt God's word, which is sinful according to Palmer.[89] This doubt can prevent sanctification from taking place. As Charles White notes, this step becomes ambiguous and problematic for some because "There is a subtle shift in the object of faith, so that one confuses trusting the veracity of God with believing something about oneself."[90] Here again, it is possible that the seeming ambiguity is only present or a problem when Palmer's shorter way is reified into a rigid, three-step event that takes place once and is primarily a legal transaction. As will become clear in subsequent chapters, what Palmer is really describing with the limited conceptual framework available to her, is what the contemplative Catholic tradition identifies as a threefold process of negation, purgation, and illumination. The seeming ambiguity of Palmer's shorter way is in fact a distinctly Wesleyan form of *via negativa* spirituality.

The third and final step of the shorter way is that of testimony. Indeed if this step is omitted, argues Palmer, sanctification cannot be retained. John Fletcher, one of Palmer's heroes of faith, reports that he lost the blessing of holiness five times because of failing to testify about it. Palmer begins the section of *Full Salvation* entitled "Publish It, Tell It" with Fletcher's experience, then goes on to describe the power of the Holy Spirit that came upon a camp meeting when a certain minister

---

and causing some to "perish in unbelief" because the only Christianity they experienced was the false faith of hypocrites. *Full Salvation*, 76. Palmer also explains that perfection is not in wisdom or knowledge, but in love—to love God with all of one's heart. In this she reflects Wesley's understanding of perfection as the teleological fullness of love of God and neighbor.

88. Ibid., 137–38.

89. White, *Beauty of Holiness*, 139.

90. Ibid., 139.

there finally began to testify to having been sanctified.[91] Several others present who had "lost the blessing" regained it as this man testified to the baptism of the Holy Spirit.[92] Citing Rom 10:9–10, Palmer urges those who have believed in their hearts to also "testify with their mouths" to the truth of what God has done. Palmer follows Wesley in this step, for he also urged Christians to tell others what God has done for them.[93]

Testimony is necessary because the goal of sanctification is complete love of God and neighbor, and central to the expression of that love is the sharing of what God has done. The good news of the Gospel is to be given away, not selfishly kept as a private blessing. No experience of God is meant simply as a private gift. Everything is to have a larger impact upon the world. "God's gifts must be *diffused* or lost," declares Palmer. "And no one enjoying the grace but will testify to the truth of this. A light put under a bushel goes out, and then it neither enlightens ourselves nor others."[94] Testimony, like the other two steps of the shorter way, is an ongoing requirement, a spiritual discipline for the rest of one's life.

Charles White proposes that Palmer "simplified and popularized John Wesley's doctrine of entire sanctification, modifying it in six different ways."[95] These changes led not only to the eventual formation of at least a dozen Holiness denominations or movements, but also to the beginning of what became classical Pentecostal pneumatology, although the non-Pentecostal denominations such as the Church of the Nazarene that point to Palmer for their theological origins have for the most part distanced themselves from the Pentecostal denominations, primarily over the issue of *glossalalia*.[96]

91. Palmer, *Full Salvation*, 60.

92. Ibid., 61–62.

93. White, *Beauty of Holiness*, 139.

94. Palmer, *Full Salvation*, 71.

95. White, "Phoebe Palmer and the Development of Pentecostal Pneumatology," 198.

96. White, *Beauty of Holiness*, 158. Donald Dayton has also published several works treating the relationship of Palmer's theology to the rise of Pentecostalism, including his dissertation which was published as *Theological Roots of Pentecostalism*. Regarding *glossalalia*, Pentecostal denominations regard speaking in tongues as the initial evidence of the baptism of the Holy Spirit, a position eschewed by non-Pentecostal holiness denominations. Interestingly, it is because of the later linkage of the phrase "baptism in the Holy Spirit" with Pentecostalism that non-Pentecostal holiness groups

The six ways in which Palmer adapted Wesley's theology to her setting in nineteenth century American culture are as follows:[97]

Following John Fletcher, Palmer identifies sanctification with the baptism of the Holy Spirit and increasingly in her later years uses the language of "baptism of the Holy Spirit" to describe sanctification. Next, she develops Adam Clarke's focus linking holiness with power. Third, she appears to stress the instantaneous over the gradual aspects of sanctification, again following Clarke. The fourth shift is in the location of sanctification in the believer's journey. Wesley emphasized "going on to perfection," with complete sanctification being the end goal. Palmer presented the shorter way of sanctification as the beginning of the way of holiness, not the goal at the end of the journey. Fifth, Palmer simplified and made more clear to her contemporaries the process of sanctification. With Palmer there were just three, easy to understand steps: entire consecration, faith and testimony. Finally, and perhaps most controversially in her theology, Palmer stresses that one needs no other initial evidence for having been sanctified other than the words of the Bible. Assurance need not be based on having one's heart "strangely warmed" or any other external, subjective manifestation.

It is my conviction that at least some of these six changes were not the intention of the Mother of the holiness movement, nor were they changes made by her. Instead, these so-called deviations from Wesley were theological trends set in motion by Palmer's interpreters, popular writers and preachers in the Methodist tradition. As Raser comments, holiness movement theology came to be shaped more by popular Methodist religious writers who came after Palmer and her contemporaries than by established theologians.[98]

Charles E. White argues that Palmer's altar theology, rather than deviating from or perverting Wesley's understanding of sanctification, is better understood as the logical conclusion of Wesley's doctrine of

---

generally prefer the terms "entire sanctification" or "being filled with the Holy Spirit" to the seemingly Pentecostal phrase "baptism in the Holy Spirit." A similar phenomenon is seen among mainstream evangelical Christians who resist using the phrase "born again" because of fundamentalist associations with the term.

97. White, "Phoebe Palmer and the Development of Pentecostal Pneumatology," 198–99.

98. Truesdale, "Reification of Sanctification," 102.

entire sanctification.[99] If, as White suggests, Palmer's theology is not a grand departure from Wesley's after all, at least not as she presented it, and if the epistemological role of mystical experience in the development of Palmer's theology has been swallowed in the "interests of instantaneousness"[100] by subsequent interpreters, it is safe to say that some of Palmer's most important theological contributions have yet to be identified. Not only does the retrieval of Methodism's own mystic bring new light to the study of Methodist theology, spirituality and history, but it opens fruitful dialogue between Methodism, Orthodoxy and Catholicism in the field of ascetical theology.

Before moving on to ecumenical considerations through a closer study of mystical experience and the role it played in Phoebe Palmer's theology, a summary of the crux of the problem is helpful. For those within holiness traditions, the most pressing existential problem has to do with the reification of Palmer's experience of entire sanctification.

Reification and A New Trajectory

Drawing from the insights of Alfred North Whitehead's "fallacy of misplaced concreteness," Al Truesdale explains that reification is the fallacy of attributing "objective substantiality to an idea or abstraction. It is the practical equivalent of hypostatize."[101] Just as in philosophy a reification fails to base thought upon concrete experience, in theology a reification of experience fails to account for the existential realities of the persons involved. In the reification of experience, in other words, one person's experience (that of Wesley or Palmer, in this case) becomes normative as *the* holy experience that is to be expected by others regardless of their personalities, life settings, spiritual traditions and so on.

According to Truesdale, Palmer's altar theology and shorter way were actually her way of breaking through what had become the reification of Wesley's experience of sanctification.[102] "Although the reification of experience had numerous contributing elements," states Truesdale,

---

99. White, "Phoebe Palmer and the Development of Pentecostal Pneumatology," 204.

100. Truesdale, "Reification of Sanctification," 102.

101. Ibid., 96 n. 2.

102. Ibid., 97.

"its center had principally to do with temporality, and secondarily with dispositional and behavioral considerations."[103]

While Wesley probably did not expect every individual to have precisely the same emotional experience he had, he did teach that sanctification as a distinct second work of grace was normative, and that some kind of affective, inner "assurance" was normative. Yet the revivalist preachers who elicited such frustration from young Palmer, who could not seem to feel what she was supposed to feel, without realizing it had reified Wesley's experience. Their message left Palmer and others with the impression that not only should a believer undergo a distinct second work of grace subsequent to justification, he or she should expect the same kind of emotional experience that Wesley had and should expect a similar time frame in which to experience sanctification. The one seeking sanctification should be prepared to wait and pray and seek God until the "inner witness" finally comes.

Unable to experience the "norm" of having her heart strangely warmed and other expected manifestations, Palmer struggled mightily to believe she could be sanctified. Her "day of days" was in fact, to use Truesdale's framework, her day of deliverance from the reification of Wesley's experience of sanctification.

Yet ironically the same phenomenon happened with certain influential figures who followed, interpreted and popularized Palmer's teaching after her death. Rather than treating her experience (including the absence of emotion and the somewhat legalistic, contractual nature of her covenant prayer) as the unique way in which Palmer found sanctification, with the principles of her shorter way interpreted accordingly, holiness writers and speakers tended to present Palmer's experience as the literal, normative way to enter into sanctification. "Naked faith in the naked word of God" became a statement for a simple, uncritical hermeneutic of Scripture instead of a description of the profound angst of "the cloud of unknowing" that Palmer experienced. The daily process of surrender and oneness with Christ of which Palmer wrote, was swallowed by instantaneousness in the interpretation of Palmer's three steps and altar theology. The shorter way became a method for certainty among its adherents, but in the process of reification something essential was lost: the role of individual personality, life history, religious

---

103. Ibid., 97 n. 3.

tradition and numinous experience in the believer's existential experience of sanctification. Because of the reification of Palmer's experience, her actual lived experience of God was misunderstood and in some ways, forgotten.

Truesdale discusses five major exemplars of reification in the nineteenth century holiness movement, including Henry Clay Morrison (1857–1942, founder of Asbury Theological Seminary), prominent evangelist Beverly Carradine (1848–1919), Martin Wells Knapp (1835–1901, co-founder of the Pilgrim Holiness Church), founder of the Pentecostal Publishing Company, L.L. Pickett (1859–1920), and William Baxter Godbey (1833–1920), well-known evangelist and author of more than 200 books. Truesdale argues that even though these men followed a different trajectory than the original teachings of the Mother of the holiness movement, their trajectory became the norm for the holiness movement. More moderate, tempered and informed voices such as that of Randolph S. Foster[104] failed to win the day.

Although at the time of her death Palmer was probably the most influential Methodist woman of her century, the author of eighteen books and numerous articles, and had enjoyed a preaching career equal to that of Charles Finney, within a few decades her name virtually disappeared from Methodist memory. While her teaching continued to spread and be interpreted in new ways, Palmer's name, life and experience became detached from her mystical theology. A variety of circumstances led to her becoming anonymous, including her own habit of not signing articles she wrote (a common practice in her day), her books gradually going out of print and the *Guide to Holiness*, the widely-circulated paper she had edited for more than a decade, ceasing publication.[105]

Charles E. Jones suggests that "the rapid disappearance of her name from common discourse served rather to strengthen her hold on the movement she had helped shape."[106] Palmer had reinvented a

---

104. Foster (1820–1903) seemed to understand the impact of personality and experience upon the subjective experience of sanctification, justification and other aspects of the spiritual life. Foster was professor of systematic theology and served as president of Garrett Biblical Institute, president of Drew Theological Seminary and was a bishop of the Methodist Episcopal Church, South. Truesdale, "Reification of Sanctification," 99.

105. C. E. Jones, "Posthumous Pilgrimage of Phoebe Palmer," 203–4.

106. Ibid., 204.

"laicized form of Methodist ministry" and in the process had offered a "formula" for assurance of sanctification," notes Jones, betraying his own Wesleyan interpretation of her work as formulaic and simplistic, the kind of interpretation that has essentially kept Palmer as a footnote in Methodist history.[107]

While she did not set out to change the structure of ministry in the Methodist church, Palmer's revival preaching, Tuesday meetings, popular theology and altar services became a new paradigm for ministry, normative for the holiness denominations that would be founded by those following her teaching.[108]

The new holiness churches, impacted by the model of camp meeting ministry, were theologically shaped by the paradigm for sanctification which had been given through Palmer. Preaching and hymnody urged congregants to be sanctified, and the steps that were to be followed were the three steps of Palmer's shorter way. Even the architecture began to reflect Palmer's shorter way and altar theology, with the mourner's bench becoming the altar rail where kneelers prayed, placing their "all on the altar."[109]

In summary, the posthumous anonymity of Palmer as well as the anti-mystical theological bias of her interpreters effectively removed the mystical foundation of Palmer's theology. Her apophatic mysticism was neither acknowledged nor seen as a major hermeneutical key in understanding her altar theology. In assigning Palmer to the margins of official Methodist history and denying the mysticism that gave birth to her powerful ministry and theology, Methodist theologians and historians have missed one of the greatest gifts the Methodist tradition has to offer the church universal. To put it another way, dismissing Palmer from the "important" and "real" history and theology of Methodism, is something like dismissing Catherine of Siena or Hildegard von Bingen from the "real" story of Catholicism. It is time for Phoebe Palmer to be restored to her rightful place as one of the great saints and mystics in the history of the church.

---

107. Ibid.
108. Ibid., 210.
109. Ibid., 206.

2

Mysticism

Mysticism as Originary Source for Theology

WHAT IS THE RELATIONSHIP BETWEEN MYSTICISM AND THEOLOGY? How can mystical experiences or texts be "tested" for legitimacy? What counts, in other words, as an authoritative mystical experience? Pondering the relationship between mystical experience and systematic theology, William Thompson argues that theological "analysis is in the service of *contemplatio* and *adoratio*, not vice versa. In this sense," Thompson writes, "I would suggest that mystical experience and contemplation occupies a certain primacy. It leads, and theology follows."[1] The writings of the saints and mystics offer a particularly critical contribution to theology when they serve as a prophetic voice, pointing theology toward a forgotten aspect of revelation or surfacing and promoting a new direction that is necessary in theology and doctrine.[2]

Thompson goes so far as to propose that "theology is called to be a form of spirituality, and indeed of mysticism in its proper sense."[3] Reflecting contemporary postmodern hermeneutical trends in which "nontraditional" voices are welcome at the theological roundtable, Thompson recommends to systematic theology the primacy of "originary" theological genres such as narrative, myth, poetry, dialogue, and drama over abstract theological treatises.[4] The "richer, many more times compact"[5] theology found in journals, narratives and biographies of

1. W. M. Thompson, *Christology and Spirituality*, 133.
2. Ibid., 126.
3. Ibid., 14.
4. Ibid., 28–29.
5. Ibid., 123.

persons such as Palmer are the immediate written expressions of these individuals' experience of God.

Like the Bible, which as sacred writ must remain of first importance to theology, these documents need to be read with a responsible hermeneutic. That is, the texts must be allowed room to breathe and speak for themselves in their own language. Their vocabulary, which is so often indirect, metaphoric, symbolic, indeed poetic, is deliberately open-ended. These texts are more like icons in the Orthodox tradition, serving as windows through which one gazes into the divine Mystery rather than tight theological treatises.[6] While the writings of mystics do not have the same authority as the biblical canon, they should be consulted as highly authoritative documents because they record the incarnational theology of Christianity's finest exemplars.

Yet the journals, narratives, poetry and biographies of the saints such as Phoebe Palmer generally have not been given primacy in theology, particularly in Protestant circles. These documents have been assigned to the realm of spirituality, which due to its alleged "subjectivity" has been viewed as less important than what used to be thought of as "objective," abstract, philosophically oriented theology. In traditional evangelical Protestant systematic theology until recently, spirituality has been sorely neglected.[7] With the advent of post-Enlightenment thought, particularly the aforementioned trends in theological hermeneutics, a new openness is emerging toward the writings of saints, mystics and martyrs as primary sources for theology.[8]

Addressing the neglect of the mystics in favor of rationalistic theology from another perspective, a feminist hermeneutic of suspicion, Grace Jantzen comments that the direct communication of the mystic with God puts the mystic in a unique position of power, which can be

6. For a thorough and visually pleasing introduction to icons and their meaning, see Ouspensky and Lossky, *Meaning of Icons.*

7. Geoffrey Wainwright's *Doxology* was the forerunner of a new trend in Protestant theology, attempting to include the work of saints and mystics as primary sources for systematic theology.

8. William Thompson argues persuasively for the importance of the emerging new-but-ancient role of the saints, mystics and martyrs in the work of theology, providing a helpful survey of the *sentire cum sanctis et mysticis* within Catholic, Orthodox and Reformed traditions as well as examples of modern theologians who incorporate this approach, such as Karl Rahner, Hans Urs von Balthazar, Yves Congar, and many others. W. M. Thompson, *Fire and Light.*

threatening to existing theological power structures in the church. Thus
the church and its agencies have worked to contain spirituality and
mysticism by controlling the conversations in which mysticism is offi-
cially discussed, who "counts" as a bonafide mystic, and how much clout
mystics can have in the academy.[9] Jantzen critiques in particular the as-
signment of spirituality to subjective, private and "female" spheres even
though the mystics themselves avoid focusing on subjective, private,
psychological states.[10] According to Jantzen the bifurcation of spirituality (including mysticism) from theology proper, separates spirituality
from social justice and political issues, from real life, in other words. The
mystics' writings, however, are deeply concerned with real life, including social justice and politics. Thus the voices of the mystics, especially
those that have been marginalized or discounted by traditional theology, must be heard afresh.[11]

In a similar manner David Tracy argues for the necessity of theology's embracing plurality and ambiguity in its own texts, particularly
listening to the voices of those who have been discounted by tradition:

> We should, above all, learn to listen to the narratives of others,
> especially those "others" who have had to suffer our otherness
> imposed upon their interpretations of their own history and
> classics.[12]

It would seem the difficulty with Palmer's sanctification theology is that
it has suffered what Tracy calls the "imposition of otherness" by interpreters who failed to truly listen to Palmer's orientation as a mystic.
Palmer, to be sure, has fared better than some other mystics in terms of
being heard as a legitimate theological voice. Within Wesleyan holiness
studies the writings of Phoebe Palmer have been treated as theology, albeit derivative and written for a popular audience. The real problem with
Palmer has been one of hermeneutics: failing to "read the mysticism" in
her theology, thereby failing to interpret her meaning adequately.

---

9. Jantzen, *Power, Gender and Christian Mysticism*, 2.

10. Ibid., 2–7. According to Jantzen this has been a problem with the formal study
of spirituality beginning with William James.

11. Ibid., 20.

12. Tracy, *Plurality and Ambiguity*, 72. Tracy is a leading proponent of postmodern
hermeneutics, with a particular sensitivity toward hearing the voices of those whom
tradition has marginalized and disempowered.

For this reason, inquiry into Palmer's sanctification theology must begin with Palmer's mystical experiences as well as the mystagogical genres which record those experiences. After having identified Palmer's mysticism, an investigation of possible sources for her mysticism is in order. From that position we will be more likely to hear her texts more fully, allowing them, in the words of Tracy, "to challenge what we presently consider possible"[13] not only in her theology of sanctification, but also in the relationship between Wesleyan holiness spirituality and wider mystical traditions in God's church.

Ambiguity Toward Mysticism in Palmer

Ironically, while Palmer's writing, particularly *The Way of Holiness*, demonstrates her fundamental mysticism, she claimed to oppose mysticism. The following statements illustrate (all italics are Palmer's):

> Any spiritual manifestation which may not, in *all its aspects*, consist with the *written Word of God*, is questionable. Never can the soul be brought into a higher state than that for which an explicit "Thus saith the Lord," may be given . . . *Apart* from the instructions of the written Word, we may not expect to be thus directed. For the Bible is *expressly* the voice of the Spirit. Neither do the Scriptures favour anything *mystical* in religion. Refined sentimentalism, or anything that the *common* mind, imbued with the spirit of Christ, may not readily apprehend, should surely be avoided; for by the most unsophisticated may these *old paths* [of holiness] be found . . . Let us not, then, by the relation of mystical experiences, favor the idea that new light, revealing a higher state than that given in the old Bible landmarks, has been revealed to us. The Bible speaks of no third state, higher than a state of holiness; it only admonishes us to go on, "*perfecting holiness* in the fear of the Lord.[14]

> Faith, I saw, was simply taking God at his word; not some mystical sound that was to burst upon my spirit's ear, confounding my senses; but the plain, written Word of God, applied to my heart through the same power, and by the same inspirations, by which it was written: that is, holy men of God spake as they

---

13. Ibid., 84.

14. Palmer, *Full Salvation*, 146–47.

were moved by the *Holy Ghost*. Consequently, the voice of the Scriptures is the voice of the Holy Ghost.[15]

I have no sympathy for mysticism in religion. Any attainment of grace, however lofty, that does not energize the soul and bring it into sympathy with Jesus in the great work of soul-saving, leading to holy activities, does not to my conceptions, reach the Bible standard of Christian holiness.[16]

It is clear from the outset that Palmer's spirituality is thoroughly Trinitarian and distinctively Wesleyan, with a well-developed pneumatology. Scripture is the direct voice of the Holy Spirit for Palmer, and all seemingly mystical experiences must yield to the authority of Scripture. Soul-saving and holy work in the world is the expected fruit of authentic spiritual experience. For Palmer any mystical encounters that lead to quietism, passivity, antinomianism, perfectionism, individualism, gnosticism, emotionalism, or other "unscriptural isms" are spurious.[17] Does this mean, however, that Palmer is against all mysticism or that she cannot be a mystic because of her rejection of what she identifies as mysticism? Hardly.

Palmer accepted and affirmed at least five forms of extra-biblical mysticism in addition to forms of mystical experiences found in the Bible such as sacred dreams and visions.[18] The kind of mysticism she attacks is antinomianism and the form of quietism that her colleague and one time disciple, Thomas Upham, began to teach.[19] Upham's doctrine proposed a "third work of grace" in which even the possibility of sinning is taken away because of the "death of the will."[20] According

15. Ibid., 188.

16. Palmer, from *Guide to Holiness*, 43, 1863: 145–47; written February 4, 1863; excerpted in Oden, 278.

17. By "perfectionism" in this context Palmer rejects teachings of absolute sinless perfection, and also rejects a certain kind of utopian perfectionism as found in John Humphrey Noyes and the Oneida colony. The term "perfectionism" had become "tainted" because of its use by utopian sects. Palmer used the term "perfection" in a positive way when speaking of Wesleyan perfection—going on to completion in love of God and neighbor. Palmer, *Full Salvation*, 147.

18. White, "What the Holy Spirit Can and Cannot Do."

19. David Bundy suggests that Palmer was actually influenced by Upham in his incorporation of Eastern Christian themes coming through the French mystics Guyon and Fénelon. Bundy, "Visions of Sanctification," 121.

20. White, "What the Holy Spirit Can and Cannot Do," 112. Upham, a Congregational philosopher, was one of Palmer's early devotees who experienced sanctification under

to some of Upham's followers, for every believer who has experienced death of the will, every desire is from God, even desires that formerly would have been sinful. It no longer matters if a believer should break one of the Ten Commandments, for even the desire to sin is now from God and will ultimately glorify God.[21] This antinomianism is the kind of mysticism Palmer rejected.

There is in Palmer's writing a decided bias against emotionalism. The plain words of Scripture were a sufficient "sign and wonder" for Palmer's faith. Her now famous maxim was: "God said it, I believe it, that settles it." Her own experience of entire sanctification only came after a long, painful and fruitless struggle to attempt to "feel" sanctified. Satisfaction came only when she realized that she must come to God with "naked faith" in the "naked Word of God," not expecting or demanding emotional experiences to confirm the reality of her surrender to God.[22] For Palmer, the insistence on visions, locutions, emotional paroxysms, and other enthusiast excesses, was an unbelieving, Pharisaical demand for signs and wonders beyond the explicit word of God. Jesus' reprimand to Thomas: "Blessed are those who have not seen and yet have come to believe" (John 20:29b), buttressed Palmer's suspicion of what she thought of as mystical emotionalism.[23] Her personality, which

---

her instruction. His increasing attraction to antinomian forms of mysticism, including publishing statements supporting the concept of the "third work of grace" and death of the will, caused a rift between himself and Palmer in the 1850's.

21. Ibid. Since as early as 1851 Palmer began to associate antinomianism with Thomas Upham, whose ideas originated with his study of Madame Guyon and Archbishop Fénelon, among other Catholic mystics, it is unlikely that Palmer was directly influenced by either of these mystics. As we shall see presently, however, she was probably indirectly influenced by both mystics through Wesley, Fletcher, Rogers, Maxwell and other "Methodist mystics."

22. *Memoirs*, quoted in Oden, 98. The phrases "naked faith" and "naked Word of God" appear numerous times in her writing. These phrases are nuanced with *via negativa* spirituality—the necessity of holding onto the God of the Bible during times of spiritual dryness and "unknowing." The phrase "naked faith" is also found in Continental spirituality, among certain seventeenth century French mystics. The link between Palmer and the French School is explored in detail later in this chapter in the section on sources for Palmer's mysticism. Orcibal, "The Theological Originality of John Wesley and Continental Spirituality," 83–111.

23. Palmer, *Full Salvation*, 47–48.

tended to be rationalistic, in all likelihood also contributed to her mistrust of mysticism.[24]

What we also see in her attacks on "mysticism" is the age-old struggle described by Friedrich von Hügel—the "fruitful collision" and "interaction" that can and do take place between what he identified as the three necessary elements of religion. In this case the struggle is between "Mysticism and Action, as respectively Intuitive and quiescent and Volitional and effortful."[25] According to von Hügel, there is always a creative tension between the three elements, with each attempting to overtake the other two.[26] In order for religion to remain whole, each element and corresponding "soul force" must have its place. Palmer's aversion to mysticism is quite simply her resistance to permitting the mystical element of Christian experience to override or supercede biblical revelation or the faithful obedience of true discipleship.

Holiness, according to Palmer, is not for an elite, mystical few. It is accessible to all believers, is grounded in Biblical revelation *and* personal encounter with God, and is expressed actively in moral and ethical behavior. Moreover, holiness is not predominantly concerned with individual piety, but is meant to empower the church to bring the world to Christ. Thus any authentic mystical experience must ultimately lead to Scriptural holiness, which is greater love of God and neighbor, as expressed in practical deeds of service done in the name of Christ.

As Oden notes, Palmer's "practical mysticism" has more than a little in common with that of Catherine of Genoa, the subject of von Hügel's landmark work on the mystical element of religion.[27] Ernest Wall makes a similar observation in 1957, writing that the parallels between Palmer

24. One could speculate that Palmer, using today's personality profile tools would prove to be an INTJ in the Myers-Briggs Personality Type schema, and perhaps a "five" on the enneagram. She tended to be perfectionistic and task oriented, "living in her head" more than in her emotions.

25. Von Hügel, *Mystical Element*, vol. 2, 392–93.

26. The three elements are the Institutional and Historical element, the Critical-Historical and Synthetic-Philosophical element, and the Mystical and directly Operative element of religion. Each element has a corresponding "soul force," writes von Hügel, which "has turned out to be necessary to religion, and yet tends to become destructive of itself and of religion in general where this soul-force and religious element is allowed gravely to cripple, or all but to exclude, the other forces and elements, and their vigorous and normal action and influence" (ibid., 387).

27. Oden, *Selected Writings*, ix.

and Catherine of Genoa are especially evident in the social action that resulted from both women's mysticism. Wall also notes similarities between Palmer, Père de Caussade and Archbishop Fénelon.[28] And as we shall see, her spirituality and experiences paralleled those of other saints and mystics. But before investigating these experiences, we should begin with a working definition of "mysticism," a task that is not without challenge.

Mysticism

It is beyond the scope of this study to provide an exhaustive investigation into the many forms of mysticism, both Christian and non-Christian, or the multiplicity of definitions. Yet a basic definition of Christian mysticism is necessary. Von Hügel's work has already been mentioned as a valuable resource. Bernard McGinn's ambitious four volume series *The Foundations of Mysticism* is among the most recent critical treatments available.[29] *Mysticism*, Evelyn Underhill's landmark study of mystics and their phenomena, continues to be a classic in the study of spirituality. William Thompson's "theomeditative" approach to spirituality and theology models an interdisciplinary effort between spirituality and theology to describe Christian mysticism with particular sensitivity to the concerns of systematic theology. In a similar way Mark McIntosh seeks to reintegrate mysticism and theology in his recent work *Mystical Theology*, with an emphasis on theological hermeneutics and mystical texts.[30] The following definition draws primarily from these sources.

Beginning with the term "mysticism," Thompson questions the choice of this term over against "spirituality" or other related words. In some ways spirituality and mysticism may be used interchangeably, he suggests, so long as both refer to the process of radical transformation of the mystic at the deepest and most originative sources of self.[31] Thompson prefers to use the term "mysticism" sparingly, reserving it

28. Wall, "I Commend Unto You Phoebe," 403–6, 407, 408.

29. McGinn is currently working on vol. 4 of *Continuity and Change in Christian Mysticism between 1300 and 1600*.

30. McIntosh, *Mystical Theology*.

31. W. M. Thompson, *Christology and Spirituality*, 5.

for: "the consciously, deeply, radically, "accomplished" living out of Christian spirituality."[32]

Tracing the etymology of the word "mysticism"(*mustikos*) within Christian traditions, McIntosh notes that in its earliest use by Christian writers, mysticism referred primarily to the full revelation of God in Christ, which has been revealed in Scripture and is discerned in the worshipping community. Graeco-Roman uses of the term *mustikos* prior to the New Testament commonly referred to hidden or secret knowledge, particularly associated with Hellenistic mystery cults. By the time of the early church the word *mustikos* seems to have been widely used to describe any kind of religious secrets.[33] The church, however, put a new twist on the idea of *mustikos* as hidden knowledge, emphasizing the unveiling of the previously hidden wisdom and plan of God. McIntosh explains:

> "Mystical," as a term, begins its Christian career by referring simply to the hidden depths of meaning in the Scriptures; it comes to refer to the meditative exegetical practices by which the Christian community encounters the meaning of this hiddenness in Christ, and then extends from the exegetical to the liturgical forms of this encounter. In these contexts the mystical also comes to refer to all teachings or doctrines that touch on the more mysterious, even difficult, points of Christian faith.[34]

McIntosh explores the gradual change in both the meaning of the word "mysticism" and the church's understanding of the role of mysticism in theology. The word "contemplation" was the choice of earlier eras, McIntosh writes, for describing transformative encounters with God, and he goes to some lengths to explain why "contemplation" served more effectively to describe mysticism. Yet throughout his work McIntosh uses the term "mysticism" rather than contemplation, perhaps as a concession to the widespread use of the word "mysticism" in contemporary dialogue on this topic. Other commentators including William Johnston, Denys Turner, and Vladimir Lossky also use the term mysticism despite its shortcomings.[35] The word "spirituality," while

32. Ibid.

33. Ibid., 42.

34. McIntosh, *Mystical Theology*, 43. This is a definition of mysticism of which Palmer would heartily approve.

35. Johnston, *Arise, My Love*; and *Mystical Theology*. Turner, *Darkness of God*. Lossky, *The Mystical Theology of the Early Church*.

useful, has its own difficulties because of contemporary usages that ascribe "spirituality" to everything from weight loss programs to Wicca.[36] Current popular culture, enamored as it is with the rediscovery of spirituality, has given this term so many applications that it cannot explicitly refer to the phenomenon described in this study as "mysticism."

Although the word "mysticism" is problematic because it has, in Rufus Jones' terms, "been out late nights and come home bedraggled,"[37] it remains the word of choice for many scholars working in the fields of spirituality and theology. Thus it is the word used in this study to describe the radically transformative experience of the Divine that is described by the great Christian mystics and saints through the ages.

Christian mysticism is not essentially about private, inner, ecstatic experiences. Rather, Christian mysticism is about the revealing of deep spiritual truth to the worshipping community through the agency of the mystics, those who have been radically and incarnationally transformed by the Holy Spirit.[38] Supernatural experiences such as visions and ecstasies are neither incontrovertible proof of mysticism nor the real substance of mysticism. Instead, the Christian mystic is one who has attained a radical degree of holy transformation at the deepest and most originary levels of being.[39] The outcome of genuine Christian mysticism is missional action in the world. Mysticism, in other words, always results in greater love of God and neighbor.

While some forms of Christian mysticism are more Christocentric and some more Pnuemacentric, to be truly Christian, mysticism must be Trinitarian and must be anchored in the church.[40] As Harvey Egan observes, "because of Jesus' essentially Trinitarian consciousness, all authentic Christian mysticism must also be Trinitarian."[41] In their discussions of the Trinitarian aspect of Christian mysticism, McIntosh and

---

36. For but one example visit the www.amazon.com web site and search for books on spirituality. As of this writing nearly 150,000 titles appear, many of which have nothing to do with the phenomenon of mysticism.

37. Quoted in Harkness, *Mysticism*, 17.

38. McIntosh, *Mystical Theology*, 6. This is actually a theme that runs throughout *Mystical Theology*, forming a basis for McIntosh's understanding of apophasis and kataphasis.

39. W. M. Thompson, *Christology and Spirituality*, 5.

40. Ibid., 9.

41. Egan, *Christian Mysticism*, 23.

Johnston emphasize the Trinitarian *kenosis*, or the perichoretic, divine self-giving as the basis for genuine *via negativa* mysticism.[42]

To be sure, there are potential difficulties with even this simple definition of Christian mysticism if all Christian traditions are included. The Trinitarian criteria for example, raise a question as to whether Quaker mystics such as George Fox, John Woolman, and Thomas R. Kelly are truly Christian mystics, since Quaker Christianity is not clearly Trinitarian in an orthodox sense.[43] Moreover, when specifying Christian mysticism as "anchored in the church," does this mean in submission to and agreement with Catholic ecclesiology, Orthodox ecclesiology, or simply that the Christian mystic affirms and honors the "one holy, catholic, apostolic church" as named in the Apostle's Creed?

These questions demonstrate that despite the best efforts of Thompson, Egan, Johnston, McIntosh and others, there are continuing challenges in articulating a concise theological definition of Christian mysticism that "fits" ecumenically and could be accepted by most Christian traditions. For the purposes of this study of Palmer's mysticism, our definition of Christian mysticism thus far will include the criteria of Trinitarian, anchored in the church, and transformational of the mystic (and church) into greater love of God and neighbor.

In addition to theological distinctions such as Pneumacentrism that shape particular expressions of mysticism there are two major forms of mysticism—kataphatic and apophatic—that are both necessary and are in some ways "opposite," yet work together in creative tension.

Apophatic mysticism refers to the *via negativa* or what is sometimes called the way of "unknowing," for God is described according to what God is not, in order to point to God's ultimately unknowable transcendence. Because God is uncreated God cannot be known or described as just one more "thing." God is much more than can be humanly understood, and despite God's self revelation through creation, the Bible and most perfectly in Christ, God remains in many ways a divine mystery to humanity. No system of theology can fully explain

---

42. McIntosh, *Mystical Theology*, 151–83; Johnston, *Arise, My Love*, 192–201. *Kenosis* is seen in Phil 2:5–11, the hymn extolling Christ's self-emptying to the point of death on the cross.

43. Peter Toon omits Quaker writers (and Jacob Boehme) from his compendium of reliable spiritual classics for this very reason. Toon, *Spiritual Companions*, 4.

God. The mystery of God is a perpetual apophasia for theology and demands humility on the part of theologians.

Spiritual advancement in the *via negativa* involves a renunciation of the ego and a detachment from all religious images, forms, created things and experiences in order to enter deeper union with the ultimately unknowable God. Apophatic mysticism is usually defined in contrast to kataphatic mysticism which is, conversely, a path of spiritual advancement in which images, forms, creation, subjective spiritual experiences, incarnation and discursive thought all lead to union with the Divine.

Contemporary discussions around apophatic mysticism hail this form of spirituality as the one most helpful in building ecumenical bridges between Christian and non-Christian religions. John Sahadat, for example, sees the *via negativa* as the mystical path that is found in all great religious traditions in the world, though each has a different vocabulary with which to describe apophasia.[44] As both a Benedictine monk and a Hindu *sannyasi* (holy man), after many years of living in India Bede Griffiths found in apophatic mysticism the necessary link for Christian-Hindu dialogue.[45] In a similar way the Jesuit Hugo Makibi Enomiya-Lasalle lived among the Japanese for decades, experiencing and writing about the relationship between Christian apophatic mysticism, Zen and Yoga.[46]

Experiences such as those of Bede Griffiths and Enomiya-Lasalle along with the use of other scholarly strategies for bridging east and west by means of apophatic mysticism, have led some contemporary scholars to diminish the importance of kataphasis or the *via affirmativa*. There is a decidedly western, dualistic tendency toward either/or thinking in regard to these two approaches to mysticism. Yet both ways are necessary in order for Christian mysticism to remain holistic and true to its roots in Scripture and tradition.[47]

At times discussion about aphophatic mysticism can itself become a bewildering "cloud of unknowing" because of the emphasis on noth-

---

44. Sahadat, "Interreligious Study of Mysticism and a Sense of Universality," 294–96.

45. Johnston, *Arise My Love*, 70–71; Egan, "Christian Apophatic and Kataphatic Mysticisms," 399. Bede Griffiths lived from 1906–1993.

46. Egan, "Christian Apophatic and Kataphatic Mysticisms," 399.

47. Ibid., 405.

ingness, dark nights of the soul, detachment, emptiness, letting go, not knowing and so forth. A surface reading of some commentators on apophatic mysticism can give the false impression that for apophatic mystics, ordinary Christian life in this concrete world is to be viewed with a kind of Gnostic disdain for bodiliness, emotion and human relationships. Yet as McIntosh demonstrates, genuine apophatic mysticism is not so much about personal, subjective, inner experiences of "darkness" and nothingness as it is about a *de-emphasis* on experience altogether.[48]

While there are many examples of apophatic Christian mystical texts, those cited most often are the works of Meister Eckhart[49] and the fourteenth century anonymous English work entitled *The Cloud of Unknowing*. Egan presents the paradigmatic *Cloud of Unknowing* in the manner suggested by McIntosh, not as an apophatic work encouraging readers to seek experiences of darkness, but rather as an apophatic mystical text that is rooted in kataphatic mysticism and grounded very much in Scripture, tradition, liturgy, ecclesiology and the felt experience of divine love.[50] Resisting the contemporary trend that downplays kataphatic mysticism, Egan concludes his discussion *of The Cloud of Unknowing*:

> In summary, the *Cloud* provides an excellent illustration of orthodox Christian, apophatic mysticism. It urges forgetting and unknowing in the service of a blind, silent love beyond all images, thoughts, and feelings, a love which gradually purifies, illuminates, and unites the contemplative to the Source of this love. Discursive meditation, self-knowledge, study, Scripture, pious practices, etc. remain the indispensable kataphatic basis for future, deeper prayer. They build the launch pad from which the apophatic thrust is correctly aimed.[51]

Kataphatic mysticism, argues Johnston, is the mysticism of the Hebrew prophets. It is a mysticism of affirmation, with God as the

---

48. McIntosh, *Mystical Theology*, 23. This insightful distinction is of particular importance in subsequent chapters treating of apophatic mysticism in Palmer's writing.

49. Eckhart, *Meister Eckhart*. Johnston, *Cloud of Unknowing*. The works of John of the Cross and Pseudo-Dionysius are also frequently cited.

50. Egan, "Christian Apophatic and Kataphatic Mysticisms," 407–9.

51. Ibid., 413.

source of all that exists.[52] God speaks to Moses in a burning bush, not in silence and nothingness. The prophet Ezekiel sees visions of God, as do Isaiah, Jeremiah, Amos and others. In the New Testament the incarnation of Jesus adds to the Old Testament foundation of the *via affirmativa*. As St. Paul writes, "He [Christ] is the image of the invisible God, the firstborn of all creation . . . for in him all the fullness of God was pleased to dwell."[53] Throughout the New Testament there are stories of mystical visions, dreams, actions, experiences and encounters. Indeed, kataphatic mysticism is overwhelmingly present in the New Testament. Thus it is safe to say that from a standpoint of Scripture alone, truly Christian mysticism must include the kataphatic.

In his attempt to keep kataphatic and apophatic mysticism together, Egan demonstrates that there is also a notable apophatic element found in the paradigmatic *Spiritual Exercises* of St. Ignatius of Loyola. These exercises have long been viewed as the ultimate example of kataphatic mysticism, with their emphasis on ascetical, discursive, emotional, sensory and imaginative forms of prayer. According to Egan, the removal of disordered loves and attachments in the Ignatian exercises is a form of apophasia.[54] Through the progressive steps of the exercises the exercitant may be led from purely kataphatic experiences of the divine, to an apophatic knowing of God as "wholly other" and beyond description. This encounter with God's transcendence is especially found in what Ignatius terms "consolation without previous cause."[55]

Texts such as *The Spiritual Exercises* and *The Cloud of Unknowing* are vital to both the study and experience of mysticism. Yet only certain mystics have the charism to write about their experiences.[56] This means that most of what has been recorded about mysticism and mystical experience has been done so by "the writing mystics," one of whom is Phoebe Palmer. Invariably these mystics not only provide descriptions of the mystic way, they write as mystagogical theologians, inviting their

---

52. Johnston, *Arise My Love*, 116–17.

53. Col 1:15, 19 (NRSV).

54. Egan, "Christian Apophatic and Kataphatic Mysticisms," 415.

55. Ibid., 419. Egan explains that this kind of consolation is given without the exercitant having done anything through acts of the mind or will to elicit the consolation.

56. Egan would drive home his point here, that the apophatic mystic's very act of writing about his or her apophasia is itself a kataphatic experience.

readers to a participatory knowing of God.[57] These texts require a particular hermeneutical stance in order to invite disclosure of their fullest meaning.

Mystical texts should not be read as descriptions of experiences that are to be slavishly imitated (particularly apophatic mysticism with its negative and dark language), but rather the texts should be seen as invitations to a new framework for any spiritual experience the reader does have.[58]

Since the original experience of mystics such as the author of *The Cloud of Unknowing* cannot be re-experienced by the reader, nor can anyone fully comprehend the interior experience of another, it is a futile endeavor, suggests McIntosh, to try to "get behind the text" to an allegedly universal mystical experience of the text's author.[59] The text itself is what is most important, for it holds the potential for becoming the facilitator of a direct experience between God and the reader.[60] Drawing from the work of Paul Riceour, McIntosh proposes that mystical texts are both sign and *res*.[61]

The mysticism described in Palmer's "theomeditative" texts should be read as both signifier and *res*. To that subject we shall address ourselves presently. But first there are a few other elements that must be added to our working definition of Christian mysticism.

Mysticism, writes Underhill, ". . . is essentially a movement of the heart, seeking to transcend the limitations of the individual standpoint and to surrender itself to ultimate Reality; for no personal gain, to satisfy no transcendental curiosity, to obtain no other-worldly joys, but purely from an instinct of love."[62] Mystics are concerned with giving, not getting, and are irresistibly drawn to become one with the Absolute.

57. McIntosh, *Mystical Theology*, 27.

58. Ibid., 135.

59. A central thesis of McIntosh's *Mystical Theology* is that the distinctive, explicit theology of various mystical texts is itself significant, that the attempt to get behind the allegedly superficial constructs of culture, religion and personality of the mystics in order to describe universal mystical phenomenon is an ill-advised project arising from post-Enlightenment Western academia. McIntosh doubts "that there *is* any such thing as spirituality or theology apart from their concrete historical life" (McIntosh, *Mystical Theology*, 5).

60. Ibid., 139.

61. Ibid., 130.

62. Underhill, *Mysticism*, 71.

In Christian mysticism, the "one-ing" process is often described as a purgative, or de-selfing journey through which one is cleansed of all that mitigates against God.[63] Moments of mystical union[64] are described with a variety of colorful metaphors: oceanic immersion, bittersweet fire, erotic embrace, and so on. With dry humor Underhill comments that the true mystic is the one who "attains to this union, not the person who talks about it."[65] This distinction is especially significant in understanding Palmer's mysticism, since she assuredly never tells her readers that she is a mystic.

According to Underhill there are four tests for true mysticism. First, it is always active and practical, an "organic life process" that reaches out into the world. Second, the goals of mysticism are wholly transcendental and spiritual, unconcerned with the advancement of self. Third, the Absolute or One with whom the mystic longs to be united, is a living and personal Beloved, drawing the soul homeward. Finally, the experience of living union with the One is a "definite state or form of enhanced life."[66]

Bernard McGinn prefers to speak of mysticism in a threefold manner: as an experience, a process, and an attempt to describe "direct consciousness of the presence of God."[67] He emphasizes, along with von Hügel that the mystical element of faith, whether in an individual or religion as a whole, is but one element. Thus the mystic is never exclusively a mystic.[68]

---

63. Again, apophatic mysticism is particularly concerned with cleansing the soul by deconstructing images of God, since God is not any *thing* (cf. Johnston, ed., *The Cloud of Unknowing*). The extreme passivity and quietism that sometimes result from apophatic mysticism were the forms of "mysticism" most vigorously protested by Palmer and by Wesley before her. Among evangelical theologians there is still a jaundiced tendency to regard all mysticism as either quietism or New Age spirituality.

64. Virtually all mystical writers agree that mystical union in this lifetime only occurs in moments that come and go. Human beings are incapable of sustained, uninterrupted intimacy. Thus the drawing toward union is a kind of dance between the soul and God, with varieties of movement and space between the Lover and the Beloved. Most importantly in this dance, the Christian mystic assures us, God is always in the lead.

65. Ibid., 72.

66. Ibid., 81.

67. McGinn, *Presence of God*, xv–xvi.

68. Ibid.

Contrary to Underhill's emphasis on union with God as the essential category of mysticism, McGinn argues for "presence" as a more useful term:

> I have come to find the term "presence" a more central and more useful category for grasping the unifying note in the varieties of Christian mysticism. Thus we can say that the mystical element in Christianity is that part of its belief and practices that concerns the preparation for, the consciousness of, and the reaction to what can be described as the immediate or direct presence of God.[69]

The mystic, then, is one for whom the immediate presence of God and the drawing of God toward unicity, is a lived, fundamental reality. God's presence is both immanent and transcendent, transforming the mystic inwardly while compelling him or her to an outward life of increasing love of God and neighbor.[70] This kind of transformation is a possibility for any Christian.

Yet the reality is that many believers do not appear to attain, in this life at least, radical transformation, thus while mysticism or mystical experiences may be found among believers who are at different levels of spiritual maturity, the one who could properly be called "one of the great Christian mystics" is much less common.

While there are great varieties of mystical experience including visionary experiences, episodes of intense numinous intuitions, spiritual combat, "dark nights of the soul"[71] and other unusual manifestations, for all mystics there is a process of growth into increasing holiness.[72] Whether the mystic is predominantly apophatic or kataphatic in his or her experience, the result of true mysticism is an ever-increasing capacity to love God and neighbor. For this reason mystics display a lover-like mixture of rapture and humility in their relationship to and language about God.[73] This is a love that is enfleshed in action. Underhill remarks: "Over and over again, the great mystics tell us, not how they speculated,

---

69. Ibid., xvii.

70. Underhill, *Mysticism*, 90.

71. A concept often linked to but not originating with St. John of the Cross and Carmelite spirituality.

72. Ibid., 75–90.

73. Ibid., 89.

but how they acted ... Their favorite symbols are those of action: battle, search, and pilgrimage."[74]

Phoebe Palmer: Mystic and Theologian

Indeed, one could scarcely find better metaphors for Palmer's approach to spiritual life than "battle, search and pilgrimage." Palmer's spiritual autobiography, *The Way of Holiness*,[75] begins with an invitation to the reader to take up the "way of holiness," a "field of investigation, boundless as eternity." Pilgrims are urged to be alert while traveling to the heavenly city for it is a journey fraught with danger:

> And yet it should not be forgotten that an enemy, subtil beyond all human conception, doth, with all his malicious agencies, his march oppose, and is ever lurking about his heavenward way ready with well-circumcised devices to withstand every step of an onward course. In view of such considerations, the Christian public will not deem an apology necessary for presenting a narrative of journeyings in the "Way of Holiness, with Notes by the Way."[76]

For Palmer the Bible was the "sword of the Spirit"[77] and the infallible guide for pilgrims, the devil a fiendish, "subtil," and persistent foe, and union with God the result of following in the Way. Palmer's mysticism was active, practical, concerned with eschatological fulfillment, process-oriented, marked with seasons of darkness and struggle, steeped in private prayer yet extraordinary in its outcome of social justice and humanitarian work. Her altar theology was much like the mysticism of Brother Lawrence of the Resurrection—a determination to "practice the presence of God" at every moment of every day, empowered by the indwelling Holy Spirit.

To illustrate let us first consider three forms of kataphatic mystical experiences Palmer had on numerous occasions. (Chapter three focuses exclusively on Palmer's apophatic mysticism.) Palmer's kataphatic

74. Ibid., 83.

75. In the preface to the 50th American edition of this work (February 18, 1867) Palmer rejoices that in a little over twenty years of the book's existence it has been translated into "both hemispheres" and read by persons in "various denominations" and foreign languages (Palmer, *Way of Holiness*, 4).

76. Palmer, *The Way of Holiness*, 5.

77. Cf. Eph 6:17; Heb 4:12.

mysticism includes visions and dreams, spiritual combat, and mystical union.

Dreams and Visions

In the twentieth century secular world the insights of Freud and Jung have given primacy to dream work as a powerful means of self-knowledge. Yet the insights of modern psychoanalysis are not new. Dreams have been honored as a source of wisdom and guidance, indeed as a means of divine-human encounter in virtually every culture in the world throughout recorded history.[78]

Patristic theologians took very seriously the role of dreams as a potential form of spiritual guidance, a mystical encounter that can be an experience of direct union with God.[79] Dreams were recognized as a key means by which God spoke to humanity in the Bible, with the New Testament alone containing at least sixteen accounts of divine communication through dreams. Because of the authority of the Bible as well as the common experience of members of the community of faith, virtually all the patristic theologians understood dreams to be a common means of divine-human encounter. Among patristic writers Tertullian leads the way in describing the spiritual significance of dreams, viewing them as the most common way God speaks to individuals.[80]

Ancient martyrs Perpetua and Felicity experienced prophetic dreams, Gregory Nazianzen was sought out for his gift in dream interpretation, and Synesius of Cyrene wrote a definitive work on dreams which is central in Greek Orthodox thought. In the west the same emphasis on dreams is found in Ambrose, Augustine, Jerome (who was converted to Christianity through a dream), and Athanasius.[81]

In a similar manner, visions are universally reported by diverse cultures in all times and places, as authentic mystical experiences. Within the Christian tradition, beyond the biblical witness, reports of visionary experiences are found throughout church history. St. Antony (d. 356),

78. Dreams, visions and other aspects of mysticism that are common to all religious traditions make the study of mysticism an exceptionally helpful bridge in ecumenical dialogue, both within and beyond Christian traditions. W. M. Thompson, *Fire and Light*, 35.

79. Kelsey, *Dreams*, 73–74.

80. Ibid.

81. Ibid., 74–77.

whose biography *The Life of St. Antony* was recorded by Athanasius (d. 1003), is prominent among the desert fathers in his reports of visions of holy ones, demons and symbolic narratives meant to unfold their meaning only after having been reflected upon for some length of time.[82] These images "are not alternatives to reason, but describe a different level of understanding."[83] With St. Antony as well as other mystics who experienced visions such as Hildegard von Bingen and Teresa of Avila, the visions are richly textured, usually requiring a substantial degree of reflection before the interpretation is clear. Fourteenth century English mystic Julian of Norwich wrote two interpretations of the same series of visions: a short version some undisclosed amount of time after experiencing the sixteen visions and then at least twenty years later, a longer version. Throughout church history, Christian visionaries have been predisposed to receive visions as authentic, Christian mystical experiences because so many visionary experiences are reported in Scripture.

Precisely because the Bible records many episodes of God speaking to people through dreams and visions, Palmer was open to her own dreams as a source of divine communication.[84] She believed, along with St. Antony, Julian of Norwich, Lorenzo Scupoli, Ignatius of Loyola and many other mystics, that demonic spirits could also communicate through dreams and visions, so she viewed these episodes prayerfully, through the lens of Scripture, in order to discern their meaning and avoid being deceived. Some of her dreams and visions were instructional, some prophetic about the future, and some a source of divine consolation.

Within an hour of having experienced assurance that she had been sanctified, Palmer describes having had a visionary experience which was her call to ministry. While in prayer, she was permitted to "enter within the veil, and *prove* the blessedness of the 'way of holiness,' that the weighty responsibilities, and also inconceivably-glorious destination of the believer, were unfolded to her spiritual vision, in a manner inexpressibly surpassing her former perceptions."[85]

82. Jones, Wainwright, and Yarnold, *Study of Spirituality*, 126–27.

83. Rousseau, "The Desert Fathers, Antony and Pachomius," 127.

84. Her brilliant defense of dreams and visions as authentic divine communications is found in *Way of Holiness*, 127–28.

85. Ibid., 34.

From her position "within the veil" Palmer saw the future unfold and saw herself as an athlete running a tremendous race. A crowd of spectators watched intensely to see how she would run. Her course was highly "fixed," and "seemed to permit of no respite, or turning to the right or to the left, and where consequences, inconceivably momentous, and eternal in duration, were pending."[86] At the same time she felt God question her about herself, about whether this kind of race could be run on her own strength or would require another kind of "exertion." The profound humility of seeing her own smallness and helplessness penetrated her mind, and she realized as never before that "it was *all* the work of the Spirit."[87] Thus the vision was one of overpowering awareness of the grace and mercy of God.

After recognizing that all holiness and spiritual capability is gift, with none of it coming from self, Palmer then heard the Spirit tell her that she was "called to profess this blessing before thousands," then questioned her, "Can you do it?" Thinking again of her own smallness and weakness, she realized how desperately she wanted to "keep the blessing" and answer the call. At that point "the Adversary" (Satan) entered the dialogue, suggesting to her that she was incapable of "keeping the blessing" and that she would surely fail. But the (Holy) Spirit came to her aid, speaking to her consolingly of the strength that would be hers in God, so she agreed to answer the call and be obedient to the vision. Afterward the Spirit brought to her mind the communion of the saints, the "great cloud of witnesses" of Hebrews 12, which strengthened her resolve to follow in the way of holiness and testify everywhere God sent her.[88] More Scriptures came to mind, as if personally given to her, especially 1 Pet 2:4–10. On the strength of this vision Palmer entered into a lifetime of ministry that was unprecedented for a woman of her day.

Shortly before her death Palmer recorded another "call" vision she had experienced in the month of August, 1840, three years after her first call vision. According to Palmer she did not speak of this visionary experience or write about it until the end of her life because she believed God did not want her to share it with "any earthly friend."[89]

86. Ibid.

87. Ibid.

88. Ibid., 36–37.

89. The vision is recorded in a document that was never published until 1988 when Oden included it in his anthology of Palmer's work. The title of the document is "Mrs.

Because of the apophatic characteristics of the 1840 experience, that vision is treated in greater detail in the next chapter. For now it suffices to say that Palmer was shown over a period of several days in a strange, dark, mysterious manner that she had been chosen to lead thousands to Christ, that she would undergo severe trials and darkness, and that she would finish her life triumphant, having walked faithfully according to her holy call.[90]

As Kate Galea argues, Palmer clearly attributed divine authority to her vision, so much so that she was willing to defy convention and enter public ministry as a revival preacher based on the authority of the vision.[91] In doing so Palmer offered a major apologetic for mysticism, regardless of what she says elsewhere against mysticism. She was willing to grant substantial authority to mystical experience as long as it could be supported biblically and it led to disciple-making and other expressions of holiness.

Just as she had foreseen in both visions, Palmer went on to preach to thousands, and testified to having been able to spend the rest of her life walking in the way of holiness, not on her own strength, but God's. Grace, not works-righteousness, became the source of inspiration for her own life and in her theology. The ability to "run the race" as she had seen in the vision came from God, not from herself. The sacrifice, she argued hundreds of times, is made holy by the altar, not by the sacrifice or the one who offers it. Jesus is the altar, and to cast oneself utterly upon Jesus, trusting in his grace, is how one is sanctified.[92] The mystical vision in which Palmer received her call to public ministry, therefore, was one of the major sources of her theology.

In a similar way Palmer experienced a prophetic dream that was fulfilled in her life and which became foundational in her altar theology. The dream is a classic example of another form of kataphatic Christian mysticism, the dream-vision:

> I thought my spirit had left the body, and entered the spiritual
> world; I found everything there very unlike what I had before

Phoebe Palmer's Testimony to the Faithfulness of the Covenant-Keeping God," dated 1875. Oden, *Selected Writings*, 322–25.

90. For a discussion of the three aspects of this call vision, see Irons, "Phoebe Palmer."

91. Galea, "Anchored Behind the Veil."

92. One of many examples may be found in Palmer, *Full Salvation*, 67.

conjectured. "What state is this?" I inquired. "This is the middle state," was the reply. "The middle state!" said I, "why, they say, on earth, there is no middle state." "They have a great many strange conjectures on earth, such as they have no *foundation for from the word of God*," was the answer. "And what is to be my state here?" I eagerly inquired. "Your state!" said the spirit, chidingly, "why you have had the BIBLE—THE WORD OF THE LORD—and by *this* you should have tried yourself, and have known what your state was before you came here; but since you have it no more with you, if you can think of but *one passage* by which to test yourself, you may just as well know what your state will be *now*, as by leaving it till you are called before your Judge, *for it is by this you are to be judged.*"

Never before did I have such a view of the infinite importance and eternal bearing of the Word of God; I saw that it was in verity as truly the word of the Lord, as though audibly uttered from the heavens, and thus arresting continuously the outward ear, as well as the inward perceptions of mortals.

I thought of the various denominations in the world that I had left, who, in expressing their doctrinal peculiarities, would say, "I believe so," and another "I believe so," and thought, "O! Why did not everyone run, with Bible in hand, raised aloft, crying 'The BIBLE says so! The BIBLE says so!'"[93]

The dream concluded with her intense struggle to remember a passage of Scripture. When she awoke the dream stayed with her for days, urging her to trust the Word of God. Yet it took several years for her to fully comprehend the significance of the dream, for she still struggled within herself to experience further "luminous or extraordinary" proofs of the presence of God. She came to see the dream as being given not only for her own edification, but also to reinforce the foundation for her altar theology and the "shorter way" of holiness, which is based on simply taking God at his word.

It is significant to note at this point that whereas Catholic mystics historically tended to have dreams and visions focusing on the incarnational Word—the sacrament of the Eucharist, the crucifix, the infant Jesus, Mary, or the sufferings of Christ—Palmer's Protestant Wesleyan heritage conditioned her to be more oriented toward the sacramental presence of God in the written (Scripture) and preached Word. Likewise, her wrestling with the demonic is subtle, intellectual

93. Ibid., 71–73.

and much concerned with Pelagianism versus grace, reflecting her personality and the Wesleyan theological milieu in which she lived. We do not find in Palmer's mystical experiences a contemplation of the crown of thorns and the withered face of Christ, for example, as the visions of Julian of Norwich, or hear Palmer describe herself as a plaything in the hands of Jesus, as does Thérèse of Lisieux. Notice, however, the similar outcome of these distinctly Catholic and Protestant Christian mystical experiences: a growth in sanctity, a deeper understanding of grace, a heightened sense of call to surrender all to Jesus, a stronger impulse to reach out to the world with God's love.

Spiritual Combat

For Palmer, spiritual warfare was a daily reality. The "Adversary" attacked frequently throughout her pilgrimage, "suggesting to her mind" that she was presumptuous for believing her call, for believing in sanctification, for engaging in public speaking, for believing in the "naked word" without signs and wonders.[94] Describing the spiritual sufferings she was called to endure as she looks back upon her life, Palmer writes:

> Yes, she was called to endure trials. To the observation of those unacquainted with the Christian warfare such a statement could hardly be understood or accredited. Consequently, the number of those who knew *just how* to sympathize was not great. Probably for this reason, in part, she seemed seldom called to dwell upon the particulars of those deep mental conflicts which she was permitted to endure, when she was called to wrestle, not against flesh and blood, but against principalities and powers, etc.
>
> These trials, though they sometimes arose from outward causes, were generally inward and the struggle they caused is indescribable; in the midst of which she was often called to lean so entirely, "with *naked* promise," that nature was sometimes tempted in its shrinkings to say, "My God, why hast thou forsaken me?"[95]

It is clear that Palmer believed spiritual combat included but was not limited to her own psychological struggles. She also believed in Satan, whom she often referred to as the Adversary, and in demonic

94. Ibid., 59.

95. Ibid., 65–66.

forces. Palmer understood these interior conflicts to involve a combination of temptation, her own scrupulousness, anxiety, and demonic oppression (the "powers and principalities and forces of wickedness" of Eph 6:12). Her conception of the mixture of human and supra-human elements in spiritual combat is consistent with the reported experiences of St. Antony, Lorenzo Scupoli, Julian of Norwich, Ignatius of Loyola, and numerous other mystics in both eastern and western traditions. Far from being "pre-critical" or naïve for their belief in spiritual combat, these mystics exhibited sophisticated insight into human nature and the relationship between psychological and spiritual healing.[96]

Jung offered the modern world a "new" (but ancient) way of understanding the combination of human, divine, and external evil spiritual realities in spiritual combat with his explanation of archetypes and the "psychoid" realm. Kelsey explains, "These can have a great impact upon those human beings who are energized by them. Archetypes are often revealed in dreams and visions."[97]

Psychiatrist M. Scott Peck offers a similar diagnosis of the presence of evil in the world and the reality of spiritual combat in his national bestseller, *People of the Lie*. Peck focuses on human evil more than demonic warfare, but he also describes his "conversion" from committed skepticism to a belief in Satan and demonic entities after having witnessed two exorcisms.[98] Hardly to be mistaken for a religious fundamentalist, Peck is convinced that people do engage in spiritual combat against the demonic, with exorcism being the most intense form of spiritual warfare. He also comments that exorcism is a form of psychotherapeutic process which brings psychological and spiritual healing to oppressed persons.[99]

It is not clear from Palmer's autobiographic statements just how much of her suffering was due to psychological distress and how much

---

96. For a recent work exploring the healing potential of Christian mysticism for the spiritual and psychological wounds of addiction, see Imbach, *Recovery of Love*.

97. Kelsey, *Psychology, Medicine and Christian Healing*, 246–47.

98. Peck, *People of the Lie*, 182–211.

99. Ibid., 185. One of his patients observes that all psychotherapy is also a form of exorcism, which makes perfect sense. It is beyond the focus of this study to provide detailed and exhaustive arguments for and against the reality of Satan as an entity. For further study the reader is referred to Peters, *Sin*; Schwarz, *Evil*; and Whitney, *What Are They Saying About God and Evil?*

was from "powers and principalities." What I propose is that these repeated bouts of "intense mental conflicts" with their sense of emotional anguish and being Godforsaken were part of Palmer's "dark night of the soul."

As Underhill explains, the dark night takes many forms and is generally suited to the temperament of the individual mystic. For those of Palmer's type—intellectual and rationalistic—the temptations of the night tend to be intellectual and rationalistic.[100] Palmer described these episodes of darkness as distinctly *mental* conflicts. She also recorded seasons of profound spiritual depression and spiritual struggle surrounding the death of her children. In these and other dark experiences, the result was purgative in Palmer's life. She emerged from each experience with a deepened sense of purpose, greater detachment towards the world and a greater sense of union with God. Thus the mystical experiences of spiritual combat brought about greater fruitfulness in Palmer's life and ministry, a sure sign of her being part of a long tradition of Christian mystics who "wrestled with dark angels."

Mystical Union

While she was generally resistant to emotionalism and sentimental religious flatulence,[101] Palmer both experienced and attempted to describe many unitive moments and visions of intense spiritual ecstasy. In doing so she used language that is the native tongue of many Catholic mystics. Images of mystical marriage to Christ, being lost in oceanic love, being filled with the fire of the Spirit, becoming one with the will of God—this is the language of John of the Cross, Teresa of Avila, Catherine of Siena, *and Phoebe Palmer*. The following excerpt from a journal entry dated July 27, 1837, illustrates:

> I felt that the Spirit was leading into a solemn, most sacred, and inviolable compact between God and the soul that came forth from Him, by which, in the sight of God, angels and men, I was to be united in oneness with the Lord my Redeemer, requiring unquestioning allegiance on my part, and infinite love and everlasting salvation, guidance and protection, on the part of Him

100. Underhill, *Mysticism*, 387–92.

101. For a recent effort to acquit Palmer of being unemotional, see Armstrong, "Ravished Heart or Naked Faith."

who had loved and redeemed me, so that from henceforth He might say to me, "I will betroth thee unto Me forever."[102]

After another wrestling match with Satan, Palmer records a decisive victory by the Holy Spirit, with descriptions of oceanic union similar to those of Madame Guyon in *A Short Method of Prayer*:

> She felt in experimental verity that it was not in vain she had believed; her very existence seemed lost and swallowed up in God; she plunged, as it were, into an immeasurable ocean of love, light and power, and realized that she was encompassed with the favor of the Almighty as with a shield.[103]

Immediately following this experience she felt an intense desire to share with "every disciple" the reality of the power of God's perfecting love, and the trustworthiness of God's word.

Thoroughly Trinitarian in her faith, Palmer describes another experience of realization of her state of dwelling in the Trinity, and the Trinity in her. She ponders the mystery of the Spirit revealing to her through Scripture, the things of God, then exclaims that the Spirit and God (the Father) enable her not only to "abide in the doctrine of Christ, but daily to become more established, and my heart is indeed made the abode of the Triune Deity."[104] The parallels with St. Teresa of Avila and other mystics, who had similar intuitions or manifestations of the indwelling Trinity are unmistakable.[105]

Unitive experiences such as those described by Palmer, are marks of the mature phase of "the unitive way."[106] The mystic who experiences such moments of union with God in prayer, also experiences intermittent seasons of longing for further oneness with God, but the longing is rooted in a deep peace and trust in God. Unicity develops as a result of the dark night of the soul: "The growth in faith, hope and love, wrought in the dark night of the soul, opens the person to the divine initiative that is symbolized in the metaphor of betrothal at the beginning of the unitive way."[107]

---

102. Wheatley, *Life and Letters*, 39.

103. Palmer, *Way of Holiness*, 31.

104. Ibid., 136–37.

105. St. Teresa of Avila, *Collected Works*, 391–92.

106. McGonigle, "Union, The Unitive Way," 987–88.

107. Ibid., 987.

The fruit of unitive experiences is a powerful desire in the mystic to help all people experience salvation and sanctification. This desire partly originates in visions of the mystic being made one with the Trinity, whose goal in the church is to seek and to save the lost. Thus the life of the mystic increasingly becomes one of humble service in the world.[108] It seems apparent that Palmer is typical of the great Christian mystics in regard to unitive mystical experiences.

Palmer's mysticism, grounded in Scripture and orthodox Christian theology, was the originary source for her theology. The reality of the indwelling Holy Spirit was to her a "tongue of fire" that was as powerful in her day as it was on the Day of Pentecost. Palmer's many experiences of the Holy Spirit were all understood by her to be a divine empowerment to be a Bible Christian.

It cannot be overstated that in Palmer's experiential, *Wesleyan* mysticism, despite having had numerous dreams, visions, episodes of spiritual warfare and moments of mystical union, the plain words of the Bible were evidence enough for Palmer's faith. Though mystical experiences carried much authority in her life, they did so inasmuch as they served to further her love for God and her obedience to God's word, the Bible. She did not demand or even recommend mystical experiences as being necessary for growth in holiness. A holy Christian is a Bible Christian, declared Palmer again and again. For her there was no other kind of authentic Christian.[109] Lukewarm, biblically illiterate "professors," argued Palmer, are the reason the world is in such a sorry state and so many people are turned off by the church. Like the great reformers before and after her, Palmer preached that a return to the way of scriptural holiness was necessary so that the world could experience the incarnate presence of Christ. Nothing less would do.

108. Ibid., 988.

109. Palmer, excerpted from *Entire Devotion to God* in Oden, 186; *Way of Holiness and Notes by the Way*, 16–17, 28, 38, 52–53, 57, 79. Palmer's writing is filled with the teaching that the Bible is to be the supreme source of faith and practice for the Christian, the Bible has authority higher than any human authority or experience, and that the Bible is the Word of God. A "Bible Christian" in other words, is one who has submitted his or her life to the authority of the Bible and who is radically transformed by the internalization of the message of the Bible. This transformation is the work of the Holy Spirit, whose "voice" is the voice of Scripture. Palmer, *Full Salvation*, 31. 74.

Sources of Mysticism

With Palmer's expressed disavowal of mysticism, we must explore how she nonetheless came to embrace classical Christian mysticism. Did she have models? Was she consciously imitating the language and experience of others, or were her experiences unique to herself, so far as she knew?

Palmer's mysticism is a practical, bibliocentric mysticism, born of a consistent lifetime of prayer and shaped by her Wesleyan heritage. But the Bible wasn't the only book that shaped Palmer's spirituality and theology. It is probable that she also read at least some of John Wesley's abridged fifty-volume edition of spiritual classics, *The Christian Library*, because Wesley prepared the library as a spiritual training course for his preachers and class leaders.[110]

Within Wesley's *Christian Library* there are eight mystical tracts and numerous other works by or about mystics, including Mme. Guyon, Francois Fénelon, Ignatius of Loyola, John of Avila (Teresa's spiritual advisor), Francis de Sales, Brother Lawrence, Gregory Lopez (who was influenced by John of the Cross), Thomas à Kempis, Blaise Pascal, Miguel de Molinos, Antoinette Bourignon, and Gaston Jean Baptiste de Renty. Each of these writers was Catholic. Wesley also included the writings of Macarius and Ephraem Syrus, two patristic mystical theologians who first interested Wesley in the notion of perfection.[111]

While it is beyond the limits of this study to treat of Wesley's relationship to mysticism in depth, it is important to note which mystics influenced Wesley, thereby influencing Palmer indirectly through Wesley and certain key followers, most notably Fletcher, Mary Bosanquet, Hester Ann Rogers, and Darcy, Lady Maxwell.

Jean Orcibal's fine study of the influence of Continental spirituality upon Wesley's theology provides a solid foundation from which to understand the sometimes stormy relationship between Wesley and mysticism.[112] For although Wesley embraced mysticism at both the beginning and end of his ministry, particularly certain mystics from the

110. Recall that Palmer was the first female class leader for a mixed gender class in New York. She does not explicitly state in her autobiography or memoirs that she read Wesley's library, but it is probable that she read some of it because of her status as class leader.

111. Tuttle, *Mysticism in the Wesleyan Tradition*, 82.

112. Orcibal, "Theological Originality," 83–111.

Bérullian School, after his failed mission to Georgia (1736) he rejected mysticism, publishing a number of polemical statements against mysticism. After about 1765, however, he spoke with increasingly positive language about the contribution and example of the mystics. By 1783 Wesley "retracted the [anti-mystical] expressions which had come from his own pen on the subject of the mystics."[113]

Wesley was first exposed to the mystics through his parents, Samuel and Susannah Wesley. Renty and Pascal were favored spiritual writers in the Wesley home, with Susannah having virtually memorized word for word Kennett's 1704 translation of the *Pensées*.[114] Beginning with his Holy Club days at Oxford, Wesley immersed himself in *The Imitation of Christ*, Jeremy Taylor, William Law, Henry Scougal, and others. Of all the mystics Renty seems to have had the most consistent impact upon Wesley, who even during his "anti-mysticism phase" regularly cited Renty in his polemic against Arianism.[115] At the end of one of Wesley's most significant theological treatises on sanctification, "A Plain Account of Christian Perfection" (1765) he includes *Instructions chrétiens*, after having edited four editions of this work by Saint-Cyran, who gathered the maxims from Robert d'Andilly.[116] Wesley claimed that *Instructions chrétiens* was second only to the Bible in terms of instruction on the way of perfection.[117] By 1776 Wesley, in describing Madame Guyon, wrote: "And yet with all this dross, how much pure gold is mixed . . . So that, upon the whole, I know not whether we may not search many centuries to find another woman who was such a pattern of true holiness."[118]

Wesley, who was accused of being a "closet Jesuit" and was likened to both St. Francis of Assisi and Ignatius of Loyola for his open air preaching and reforming tendencies, demonstrated remarkable theological acumen in his integration of diverse theological voices, including those of numerous mystics. His theology of justification, sanctification and perfection were all informed by the writings of the mystics, particularly

---

113. Ibid., 95.

114. Ibid., 89.

115. Ibid., 90.

116. Bautz, "Robert d'Andilly Arnauld."

117. Orcibal, "Theological Originality," 103.

118. Ibid., 94.

those of the Bérullian School.[119] Orcibal concludes, "According to Cell's formula, which has won the assent of the best historians, Wesley was conscious that his teaching was 'the necessary synthesis of the Protestant ethic of grace and the Catholic ethic of holiness.'"[120]

Palmer, it is safe to say, as a good Methodist class leader probably read at least some of Brother Lawrence, Gaston de Renty, and the other mystics in Wesley's abridged editions. She also shared a sometimes turbulent but long-term friendship with Thomas Upham, who edited best-selling abridgements of the life of Madame Guyon and Archbishop Fénelon.[121] In Bundy's estimation, Palmer and Upham, more than any other holiness theologians, were responsible for the shift in Wesleyan sanctification theology, a changed emphasis that reflected the mystical influence of Guyon and Fénelon, as well as Wesley's mysticism reinterpreted through John Fletcher.[122]

Another close friend, Timothy Merritt, founder of the publication *Guide to Holiness* (for which Palmer eventually served as editor for over 10 years), wrote *The Christian's Manual: A Treatise on Christian Perfection, with Directions for Obtaining That State* (1825). The manual heavily cites both Wesley and John Fletcher, whose name appears frequently in Palmer's writing. Fletcher was, in the eyes of Palmer, as sainted as Paul the Apostle or any of the patristic writers.

Fletcher's spirituality was steeped in the Bible, *The Imitation of Christ*, Brother Lawrence and several books by or about Madame Guyon. It was said that, "when the atheist philosopher Voltaire was asked who was the most Christ-like person in the modern world, he replied without hesitation, 'John Fletcher of Madeley.'" In Wesley's funeral sermon for Fletcher, he remarked that John Fletcher was the holiest man he had ever met or expected to meet this side of eternity.[123]

It was primarily through Fletcher's biography, written by Wesley with a great deal of material from Mary Bosanquet (Fletcher's wife),

119. Ibid., 108–9.

120. Ibid., 102.

121. Even though she sharply disagreed with Upham concerning what she felt were Guyon's and Fénelon's quietistic tendencies, her critique of Guyon and Fénelon had to do with what she felt was their neglect of the Bible rather than their mysticism per se. White, "What the Holy Spirit Can and Cannot Do," 112.

122. Bundy, "Visions and Sanctification," 117.

123. Jeffrey, *Burning and Shining Light*, 349.

that Palmer came to know the life and teachings of Fletcher. In Fletcher, along with previously mentioned Catholic writers, Palmer read descriptions of mystical union as marriage to Christ,[124] as being a drop of water lost in the sea of love, and as good and evil being swallowed up by grace.[125] Fletcher's sermon on the "violence which the kingdom of heaven suffereth" seems to be a clear source of inspiration for Palmer's use of the phrase in reference to spiritual warfare in *The Way of Holiness* (138–39).[126]

In addition to being influenced by Fletcher, Palmer greatly admired Mary Bosanquet Fletcher, the extraordinary woman Fletcher married when he was 52. Mary, an eloquent preacher and exceptional Bible teacher, was a role model for Palmer, who describes her as a modern Priscilla or presbyteress or female confessor of apostolic times.[127] Had Mary been Catholic, Palmer adds, she would probably have been canonized as a saint.[128]

The memoirs of Hester Ann Rogers (1756–1794) were another strong formative influence on Palmer, possibly because of certain parallels in their lives,[129] but also because of the high esteem in which Rogers was held among Methodists of Palmer's day. Having suffered much persecution along with other early Methodists in Britain, being a close friend of both Wesley and Fletcher, and having died at the young age of 39 as a result of complications from childbirth, Rogers was one of the great female heroes of faith for Methodists of Palmer's generation. It is unquestionable that Rogers influenced Palmer's interpretation of her own experiences and spiritual journey. For example in reading Rogers' memoirs Palmer would have resonated with Rogers' difficulty

124. Ibid., 366–67.

125. Ibid., 384. Unitive imagery and language such as oceanic love may be traced back to the Bérullian School, found in Renty and others. The phrase "naked faith" is another term common in Continental spirituality which was probably handed on through Wesley, Fletcher, Rogers and others to Palmer. Orcibal, "Theological Originality," 87, 88.

126. Fletcher, "Kingdom of Heaven Taken By Violence," 261–62.

127. *Promise of the Father*, 101.

128. Palmer goes to great lengths to describe the gifts and ministry of Mary Bosanquet, including Wesley's affirmation of her call to ministry. Ibid., 101–10.

129. Both lost children and struggled with guilt and depression as a result. Both struggled to experience assurance of sanctification. Both women were involved in class meeting leadership, although Rogers' husband was a minister.

in weeping as she sought assurance of salvation.[130] Rogers prayed to be "baptized with the Holy Spirit and the fire of pure love," language that is found also in Palmer.[131] Palmer's habit of reading the Bible on her knees may well be an imitation of Rogers, who followed the same practice and urged others to do so.[132] The letters of counsel found at the end of Rogers' memoirs are similar in content and style to those written later by Phoebe Palmer.

Of particular theological significance is Rogers' statement in a letter to her cousin in which she writes: "I feel I am very unworthy, yet offering up myself and my services on that altar which sanctifieth the gift, my God accepts a worthless worm, through his beloved Son."[133] In this phrase Raser sees Rogers as the contributor of "the seed" of Palmer's altar theology.[134]

Rogers records several mystical experiences in her memoirs. These include arguments with Satan in which she refutes the evil one with arguments from Scripture, experiences of union in which the language of oceanic love is used, a prophetic dream of an acquaintance (which comes to pass literally just as the person dreamed), the mystical dream of a cousin, and the life-changing mystical dream of her father.[135] At one point Rogers quotes Renty in regard to experiencing the fullness of the presence of the Trinity.[136] Each of these experiences has parallels in Palmer's autobiography, though Palmer does not directly quote Renty.

Along with the memoirs of Hester Ann Rogers, one of the other chief influences upon Palmer's spiritual formation was the biography of Darcy, Lady Maxwell (ca. 1742–1810). Lady Maxwell, who was a close friend and disciple of John Wesley, lived most of her life as a widow. After two brief, but happy years of marriage her husband Walter died, followed by the death of their only child just six weeks later. Because of the deaths of her husband and young son, Maxwell devoted herself to God in service for the rest of her life, never speaking of her deceased

---

130. Rogers, *Account of the Experience of Hester Ann Rogers*, 28.

131. Ibid., 43.

132. Ibid., 33.

133. Ibid., 188.

134. Raser, 247.

135. Rogers, *Account of the Experience*, 5, 28, 37, 156–57, 64–65.

136. Ibid., 52–53.

family again, only allowing the grief to draw her into deeper communion with God and to a life of serving others. As Maxwell often said: "God brought me to himself by afflictions."[137]

Palmer's interpretation of her three children's deaths and her angst over possibly loving her own husband too much, are similar to Maxwell's. Like Palmer after her, Maxwell wrote a prayer of surrender when she received "full salvation,"[138] and kept an extensive spiritual journal. Descriptions of her devotional practice are paralleled in Palmer's journals, indicating the likelihood that Palmer followed Maxwell's example in attending to the means of grace.[139] Both women were financially able to support a variety of ministries to help the poor and both women used their upper-class social standing as a means to work for social justice.

Throughout her life Maxwell testifies to having mystical experiences such as spiritual warfare against the Adversary and visitations of the Deity, but these become more frequent as she draws closer to death. Numerous times she records visitations of the Trinity and of holding discourse with Father, Son and Spirit in a manner beyond words.[140] It is clear throughout her memoirs that prayer is the central focus of her life.

While there were undoubtedly other influences upon Palmer and her openness to "biblical" mysticism, Wesley, Fletcher, Bosanquet, Rogers, and Maxwell seem to be the most important in terms of the number of times they are mentioned in Palmer's work, and the similarities in mystical experiences and language. While all of these were staunch Methodists, all of them were directly influenced by Catholic mystics. Their internalization of Renty, Brother Lawrence, Guyon and others was handed on to Palmer, whose theology and ministry emerged from her own mystical experiences.

Conclusion

Thomas Oden notes that Palmer would be "amused" to hear herself referred to as a theologian.[141] She would be agitated to hear herself called

---

137. Lancaster, *Life of Lady Maxwell*, 13.

138. Ibid., 21.

139. Ibid., 9–30.

140. Ibid., 377.

141. Oden, *Selected Writings*, 14.

a mystic. Palmer regarded herself as a simple woman who was a "Bible Christian." Theology, in Palmer's opinion, was what hindered her for a very long time from entering into the way of holiness, for she had occupied herself with endless "theological hair-splitting."[142] The lack of spirituality of so many theologians, preachers and "professors" served as a goad that spurred the urgency of her message. When asked to pray at the dedication of Garrett Biblical Institute in May, 1869, she said:

> May this school of the prophets ever be a praise on the earth not only for literary advantages and soundness of creed, but for richness of divine unction; or in other words, for the reception of the full baptism of the Holy Ghost, on the part of all who, in coming time, shall be trained within these walls for the holy ministry. Surely, a holy work demands, first of all, a holy heart.[143]

Phoebe Palmer's mysticism—her lived experience of the transforming presence of God—gave birth to her theology which had an incalculable impact on the world. Palmer's achievements as a preacher, humanitarian, ecumenist, feminist, writer and theologian were all due to her grounding in "the mystical element of religion." Palmer's mystical experiences and their powerful impact on her ministry are clearly within the stream of a long tradition of Christian mysticism.

Thomas Oden suggests many reasons that Palmer is a theologian for our time. I believe that Palmer is also a mystic for our time. She is a patron saint for those who would bring reformation to Methodism in decline. Palmer was able to adapt Wesley's theology and solid biblical teaching to her culture in a way that both reached the people and maintained the integrity of the Gospel.[144] As a theologian she drank deeply from many springs. Her theology was for the church, to bring the church into the "way of holiness." For Palmer, as for St. Paul and Jesus himself, true theology is holistic. Theology is about ordinary people discovering and living into the incredible Good News. It seems fitting to close this chapter with a comment penned by the Mother of the holiness movement, which she intended for those who would be theologians and other kinds of "professors." It is the observation of a Christian mystic:

142. Palmer, *Full Salvation*, 187–88.
143. Oden, *Selected Writings*, 299.
144. Ibid., 5.

Don't aim too high, for the benefits of getting down low are incalculable. Everything in religion is exceedingly simple.[145]

145. Palmer, *Full Salvation*, 46.

3

The *Via Negativa*

Introduction

IN THIS CHAPTER WE WILL FOCUS ON APOPHATIC MYSTICISM AS FOUND in Palmer's life and writing.[1] This exploration of Palmer's *via negativa* spirituality builds upon the foundational assertion of McIntosh and others that the *via negativa* is concerned with a de-emphasis or relativization of experience rather than an emphasis on experiences of darkness, nothingness, or emptiness. As already discussed in the previous chapter, experientialism is by definition kataphatic. While experiences of negation, darkness, loss, or self-emptying are part of the *via negativa*, the primary focal point for apophatic mysticism is God rather than personal experiences of God. Experience, emotion, affectivity are all part of incarnational faith, thus it is to be expected that a genuine Christian faith journey will include religious emotion and experience. Apophatic spirituality cannot stand alone and remain healthy or "normal" in the sense of being an accurate expression of truly Christian faith, since Christianity is incarnational. Christian apophatic spirituality does not eliminate experience and emotion, rather it relativizes the place of experience and emotion. Thus the following discussion takes into account Palmer's descriptions of her personal experiences of negation and darkness, but the overall trajectory both in this discussion and in Palmer's writing is her general de-emphasis on affective experience in order to embrace the Holy.

---

1. This chapter was originally published in slightly different form as "*Via Negativa* in the Life and Thought of Phoebe Palmer" and is included with permission of the publisher.

At least three aspects of apophatic mysticism can be found in Palmer's autobiographic records. These are: the struggle to accept internal "darkness" and "nothingness" in order to enter the way of holiness or oneness with God; the ongoing experience of "passive" surrender to God leading to progressively advanced spiritual development, and dark nights of the soul as a purgative initiation into deeper levels of union with God. As we shall see, Palmer's apophatic mysticism was at the core of the pivotal events in her spiritual journey, becoming the fountainhead for her most significant contributions to Wesleyan theology.

Naked Faith in the Naked Word

The first indicator of Palmer's apophatic mysticism came in her early years as she struggled for assurance of sanctification. Having grown up in a devout Methodist household, Palmer was exposed to Methodist revivalism from infancy and made a genuine faith commitment at age four.[2] This revivalism was aimed at "lukewarm Christians" and stressed the need for a "second work of grace," through which the believer is sanctified for a life of holiness. Following the model of John Wesley's Aldersgate experience, Methodist revivalists preached that the second work of grace was affectively marked by an "inner witness of the Spirit," testifying within oneself that sanctification had taken place.[3]

As we have seen, influenced by such preaching, Palmer struggled mightily through her teen years to experience an inner conversion marked by a changed "feeling," yet the feelings would not come. Like many who make authentic faith commitments as young children, Palmer could not remember *not* walking with God. Yet the sense of a divine call to deeper holiness persisted.[4] Palmer describes finally reaching a crisis point in which she felt she either had to experience the "second work" or lose her salvation:

> Others may act upon the principle that it is optional with themselves whether they will remain in a state of justification, or go on to a state of entire sanctification, but, with me, the command was absolute, "Go on to perfection"—"be ye holy"; and, if I had

2. Pamler, *Way of Holiness*, 49.

3. There is a parallel to later forms of Pentecostalism that insist upon the manifestation of speaking in tongues as proof of baptism of the Holy Spirit.

4. Palmer, *Way of Holiness*, 49–53.

not obeyed, how could I have been in a state of condemnation and in a state of justification at the same time?[5]

For Palmer "entire sanctification" meant utterly giving over to God everything she was, everything she had, all her relationships, dreams, hopes, and especially her will. It meant putting herself on the altar of Jesus[6] to be a living sacrifice, an "eternal surrender of life, reputation, and friends dearer than life."[7] The life of surrender was, for Palmer, "the way of holiness."[8]

The crux of Palmer's struggle was her inability to experience sanctified "feelings," strive as she might. In other words, her lack of kataphatic experience produced great anxiety in the young seeker of holiness. No amount of good works, prayer, anxiety or thought could produce the desired affective awareness that she was one with God, given over to live in one accord with God's will. Again and again as she wrestled with absence of feeling, she felt Satan tempting her with the accusation that she was presumptuous for even thinking she could be holy.[9]

In this struggle I propose that Palmer was experiencing the affective "nothingness" that is part of apophatic mysticism. She felt intense and unremitting desire (*erōs*) for oneness with the God who seemed to have become affectively absent. I further suggest that Palmer was, in the schema of Francis Nemeck and Marie Coombs, passing through one of seven "critical thresholds" along the way to the mature spiritual development of a contemplative.[10] A "critical threshold" is a major spiritual

---

5. Palmer, *Full Salvation*, 26.

6. Recall that Palmer's concept of Jesus as the altar that consecrates the gift is the foundation of her "altar theology," her most notable contribution to the development of Wesleyan theology. It is based upon her interpretation of Heb 13:10.

7. Palmer, *Full Salvation*, 27.

8. Amanda Portersfield proposes an incipient female eroticism in Palmer's language about "laying" oneself on the altar in order to surrender passively to God. Portersfield's suggestion is interesting especially in light of the spiritual eroticism of other female mystics such as St. Teresa of Avila. Amanda Portersfield, "Phoebe Palmer," 11.

9. Palmer, *Way of Holiness*, 82.

10. Nemeck and Coombs, *Spiritual Journey*, 48. Nemeck and Coombs have written extensively on the spirituality and apophatic mysticism of St. John of the Cross, including in this book. According to the authors there are 7 major thresholds in the development of most contemplatives (*Spiritual Journey*, 33–38). Personal conversion is the fourth threshold. While the authors use the designation of one who enters the "blessed night" as a "contemplative" rather than a "mystic," their term "contemplative" means approximately the same thing that is meant by the term "mystic" in this study.

change marked by three qualities, explain Nemeck and Coombs. Critical thresholds are radical, irreversible and successive. The contemplative is radically changed, never goes back to the way he or she "used to be," and the thresholds are progressive over the course of the contemplative's lifetime.[11]

The threshold which Palmer seems to have been experiencing at this point is described by Nemeck and Coombs as that of "personal conversion," a subset of a larger category they name "emergence":

> *Personal conversion* is a special modality of emergence. It is a singular moment in our lives. Emergence and personal conversion go together like two sides of the same coin. "Emergence" denotes not only a threshold but also an élan which endures for the rest of our lives. "Personal conversion," on the other hand, designates a unique instant of breakthrough and definitive stabilization in the process of emergence. From that moment on, we realize that we are possessed by Christ and that we wholeheartedly desire to surrender ourselves to him in love, hope and faith.[12]

The definitive breakthrough came for Palmer on July 26, 1837, the "Day of Days" when she made her irrevocable "altar covenant" with God.[13] Palmer's breakthrough came as a result of her realization that holiness was promised to her by God's Word and that promise was true regardless of her emotions. Palmer came to view her previous demand for an emotional "proof" of sanctification as being like the sinful demand of the Pharisees for Jesus to produce ever more "signs and wonders" before they would believe his words. At the same time, Palmer was seized with a deepened conviction that she had to relinquish what she felt to be an excessive attachment to her husband and children.

As Nemeck and Coombs note, thresholds are often precipitated by personal trauma such as serious illness, major personal failure or loss of a relationship through disruption or death, an observation that is true of Palmer.[14] Grief over the deaths of three of her children, particularly Eliza who died exactly one year before her experience of sanctification,

---

11. Ibid., 33–34.
12. Ibid., 48.
13. Oden, *Selected Writings*, 114.
14. Nemeck and Coombs, *Spiritual Journey*, 35.

led Palmer to conclude she had loved her family idolatrously.[15] She felt
a divine imperative to detach from her family in the Ignatian sense of
"a removal of disordered loves and attachments."[16] So it was that as
she relinquished both the demand for affective proof of sanctification
and her "idolatrous" attachment to family, Palmer finally entered into
sanctification—the state of simple, undivided rest in God—for which
she had longed.[17]

Palmer experienced the necessary detachment of the *via negativa*:
the letting go of people, created things, religious feelings, and her own
will in order to embrace the God who is wholly other. She entered into
quietness of soul by means of the *via negativa*, rather than through
kataphatic experiences of having her heart "strangely warmed" as John
Wesley did, or some other affective experience.

Thus Palmer entered into apophatic mystical passivity in precisely
the sense described by von Hügel: a quietness of soul brought about by
the activity of bringing all of one's faculties into harmony with God.[18]
And, as is true of other great mystics of the Church, Palmer's experience of passivity became the fountainhead for a lifetime of missional
service.[19] Palmer's apophatic "Day of Days" was the ultimate source
of authority for her unprecedented move into public ministry which
involved preaching, teaching, writing, humanitarian work and international travel.

Mystical Passivity: Quiet or Quietism?

The experience of mystical passivity is part of the *via negativa* in that it
has to do with divinely initiated movements of the soul toward a greater
reception of grace and a diminished reliance upon self. Both passivity
and darkness are purgative of the soul's fallen tendency toward self-
absorption. The experience aptly named the "dark night of the soul" by
St. John of the Cross, is one which usually leads souls into experiences

15. Palmer, *Full Salvation*, 145–46; *Way of Holiness*, 151–52.

16. Egan, "Christian Apophatic and Kataphatic Mysticisms," 415.

17. Oden, *Selected Writings*, 114–22.

18. Von Hügel's explanation of mystical passivity is treated at length in the next
section of this chapter, beginning on the next page.

19. Recall that within an hour of having assurance of her sanctification, Phoebe
describes having a visionary experience that was her call to ministry. Palmer, *Way of
Holiness*, 34.

of passivity, for the lesson that is learned in the night is that one's efforts to be holy on one's own strength are ultimately doomed.

Holy simplicity, the prayer of quiet, the deep rest of cessation from feverish striving: these gifts are imparted by God to souls who meekly surrender to God and *receive*. Union with God is the result of grace alone. Yet, as von Hügel argues at length, the state of the soul at rest that is called "passivity" is in fact quite active. Quiet, in other words, is not Quietism.

The biggest distinction that must be made in defining authentic, orthodox experiences of "mystical passivity" is that between "quiet" and "Quietism."[20] This distinction is of particular importance in evaluating the apophatic experiences of Palmer and her own understanding of them. For, as already discussed elsewhere, Palmer was adamantly opposed to Quietism, which she thought of as mysticism.

What, then, is "quiet" as opposed to Quietism? Throughout the history of Christian spirituality there have been two currents, to borrow von Hügel's image, in regard to mystical passivity.[21] One of the currents emphasizes the soul's simplicity as an increased quietude involving cessation of effort of the self toward God so as to more openly receive grace. This quietude is experienced most notably in prayer. "Its decisive terms are Passivity, Fixedness, Oneness," writes von Hügel.[22]

The other current understands the reception of grace as a collaborative effort between the soul and God, such that it requires the constant "action" of cooperating with the latent, Spirit-borne impulses toward holiness that arise from within the soul. "Its characteristic terms are "Action" (as distinguished from "Activity"), Growth, Harmony."[23] The two currents belong together and serve to balance each other. Yet von Hügel stresses the underlying reality that human response and activity are always required in true mystical passivity. In other words, both currents involve Action.

Borrowing from Aquinas' concept of God as Pure Act, von Hügel explains that when the soul experiences passivity in prayer, that is, it seems to have "lost itself in God" or ceased to be distinct from God dur-

---

20. Quietism has been regarded within Christendom almost exclusively as a heterodox phenomenon.

21. Von Hügel, *Mystical Element of Religion*, 131.

22. Ibid.

23. Ibid.

ing moments of mystical union or at advanced stages of prayer, the impression is only an appearance. The same is true of passivity in terms of an hour-by-hour lived experience of resting in God while going about one's work, as in Brother Lawrence's experience of the "practice of the Presence of God." In actuality, the:

> . . . impression of rest springs most certainly from an unusually large amount of actualized energy, an energy which is now penetrating and finding expression by, every pore and fiber of the soul. The whole moral and spiritual creature expands and rests, yes; but this very rest is produced by Action "unperceived because so fleet," so near, so all fulfilling; or rather by a tissue of single acts, mental, emotional, volitional, so finely interwoven, so exceptionally stimulative and expressive of the soul's deepest aspirations, that these acts are not perceived as so many single acts, indeed that their very collective presence is apt to remain unnoticed by the soul itself.[24]

A variety of descriptions of passivity have been offered by the mystics. These descriptions vary according to the temperament of the individual mystic. St. Teresa of Avila speaks for the more passionate types when she describes the Orison of Quiet as a kind of:

> ". . . sleep of the powers of the soul" in which the soul does not know what to do—for it knows not whether to speak or be silent, whether it should laugh or weep. It is a glorious folly, a heavenly madness, wherein true wisdom is acquired; and to the soul a kind of fruition most full of delight.[25]

St. Teresa goes on to describe the utter captivation of the soul by God's love at such times, which makes it difficult to be distracted from God or to rouse oneself to activity. Passivity in prayer, then, becomes the adoring gaze of the lover upon the Beloved.

It is clear from St. Teresa's description that this kind of passivity cannot be associated with an Eastern form of detachment from all passion, selfhood, etc. On the contrary, Teresa's passivity is the enraptured, passionate absorption of the soul with God, a condition nuanced with a kind of spiritual eroticism. Such prayer is a form of "passivity" that

---

24. Ibid., 132.

25. Quoted in Underhill, *Mysticism*, 326. Originally found in St. Teresa of Avila, "*De Quatuor Gradibus Violentae Charitatis,*" col. 1215 b.

seamlessly leads into true contemplation, which subsequently bears the fruit of holy activity in the world.

The result of true mystical passivity is an increase of strength and spiritual energy, an increase of love for God and neighbor so that the individual is increasingly alive to God in the community and world as the process of passivity progresses.

Authentic mystical passivity is a de-selfing process, yet paradoxically brings about a deepening of authentic self-actualization. For this reason "healthy" passivity is a normal part of Christian sanctification.

In von Hügel's estimation the real culprit that distorts "quiet" into Quietism, is any tendency to extreme dualism, particularly between body and soul.[26] Such dualism inevitably leads to a devaluation of bodily experience, creatureliness, the historic and institutional elements of faith and community, vocal prayer and devotional practices. Dualism between soul and body devolves into a focus on the soul transcending the body, a self-abnegation that depreciates incarnationality. Dualism leads to the pursuit of a solitary journey of the soul to the great, impassable and unknowable Other, in short, a Plotinian "flight of the alone to the Alone."[27]

Quietism tends to pursue passivity as an end, rather than a means. Furthermore, argues von Hügel, such an impulse invariably becomes preoccupied with the nature of God in Godself, apart from creation.[28] Thus it becomes a direct contradiction to the fact of the Incarnation of God and of God's self-revelation exclusively within the economy of salvation. For this reason Quietism was rejected as heresy in the seventeenth century,[29] because in von Hügel's words, "God's action does not

26. Ibid., 135.

27. Louth, *Origins of the Christian Mystical Tradition*, 51.

28. An exercise in futility which has, nonetheless, dominated western Trinitarian theology from the time of Augustine, according to Catherine Mowry LaCugna. The only way humanity has ever known God is through God's self-revelation in the *oikonomia*. The notion of knowing God in *se* apart from creation is a philosophical myth. LaCugna, *God For Us*, 1–8.

29. Quietism was so named by Cardinal Caraccioli, Archbishop of Naples, in his June 30, 1682 letter to Pope Innocent XI (Odescalchi) in which he described the phenomenon of Quietism as it appeared in his Diocese. Quietist offenders had forsaken the rosary, genuflection, making the sign of the Cross, the Eucharist and other devotional practices. Spanish priest Miguel de Molinos was put on trial for two years, imprisoned and tortured for disseminating Quietist teaching from 1685–1687. Others accused of Quietism included Archbishop François Fénelon (d.1715) and his friend,

keep outside of, nor does it replace, man's action; but it is—Our Lord Himself has told us—that of yeast working in meal, which manifests its hidden power in proportion to the mass of meal which it penetrates and transforms."[30]

With this preliminary understanding of mystical passivity (quiet) and its distinction from Quietism, then, let us turn to the Mother of the holiness movement to explore the theologically formative influence of her experiences of mystical passivity.

Moments of Mystical Union

Numerous descriptions of mystical prayer are found in Palmer's writings, including classic descriptions of ecstatic passivity such as we have considered in St. Teresa of Avila. One such experience of oceanic love, so common to Catholic saints and mystics, generated within Palmer an intense desire to lead other disciples of Jesus to entire sanctification:

> She felt in experimental verity that it was not in vain she had believed; her very existence seemed lost and swallowed up in God; she plunged, as it were, into an immeasurable ocean of love, light and power, and realized that she was encompassed with the favor of the Almighty as a shield.[31]

On another occasion Palmer described her profound desire to lie passively in the hands of God, with her will lost in God's will:

> In reference to my future course, I wish to lie passive in the hands of the Lord, as an instrument to perform His pleasure in all things. My will is lost in the will of God. I would not—dare not choose for myself, though the choice were given. God is my all in all. I walk by faith, and am enabled to endure as *seeing* the Invisible, and my enjoyment consists in a calm, quiet resting on the promises of the gospel, assured that it is my Father's good pleasure to give me the kingdom. I feel at rest in the blessed persuasion, that if I, as a worker together with him, make use of the means ordained for my advancement thitherward, the point will be gained. *I know that the Holy Spirit has been given, the*

Madame Jeanne-Marie Guyon (d. 1717), whose spirituality greatly influenced Fénelon. "Fénelon, François"; "Guyon, Madame Jeanne Marie"; and "Quietism" in McBrien, ed., *HarperCollins Encyclopedia of Catholicism*, 525, 597, 1075–76.

30. Von Hügel, *Mystical Element of Religion*, 136.

31. Palmer, *The Way of Holiness*, 31.

Comforter has come! and has taken His abiding residence in my heart—inciting me ceaselessly to every good word and work, and giving me a longing desire for the spiritual benefit of those around me.[32]

Within this passage alone we find numerous elements of mystical passivity at its "best" in terms of von Hügel's description of healthy mystical passivity. Palmer describes her will being lost in the will of God, yet there is a distinct, even ennobled sense of self. She has lost neither her personality nor her freedom of choice. Palmer's experience of God's goodness and rest is not an end in itself, but becomes the means of spurring her on to share God's love with others.

Note also the manner in which Palmer's apophaticism remained grounded in Scripture, tradition and the church. In referring to the necessity of using "the means ordained for her advancement" Palmer acknowledged the importance of attending to the Wesleyan "means of grace": prayer, Bible reading, corporate worship, and the Eucharist. Unitive experiences of passivity thus led Palmer to a deeper rootedness in Scripture, the sacraments, the Church and a more effective ministry in the world.

One final example, also drawn from the "Day of Days," links Palmer's mysticism to that of St. Teresa of Avila and numerous other mystics who experienced divine betrothal as a complete surrender of the self to God. As Nemeck and Coombs comment regarding the already described "critical threshold" experience of conversion, it usually leads to the next stage of "divine espousal."[33]

I felt that the Spirit was leading into a solemn, most sacred, and inviolable compact between God and the soul that came forth from Him, by which, in the sight of God, angels and men, I was to be united in eternal oneness with the Lord my Redeemer, requiring unquestioning allegiance on my part, and infinite love and everlasting salvation, guidance and protection, on the part of Him who had loved and redeemed me, so that from henceforth He might say to me, "I will betroth thee unto Me forever."[34]

32. Ibid., 89.

33. Nemeck and Coombs, 48.

34. Oden, *Selected Writings*, 118.

In the ensuing interaction with God, Palmer surrendered herself unconditionally to mystical union on God's terms, acknowledging the probability that union would involve seasons of walking by sheer faith, trusting in the "naked word of God" in the perceived absence of spiritual passion or emotion. And that, in fact, is what she went on to experience.[35]

Mystical Passivity and the Practice of the Presence of God

As an ambassador of God to thousands of seekers of holiness, Palmer preached a "shorter, simple way," one not dependent upon emotions or other signs, but entirely upon the trustworthiness of God's word and the efficacy of Christ's atonement. According to Palmer, once a believer "lays it all on the altar" of Jesus, his or her one primary task is to trustingly abide there, moment by moment. Like Brother Lawrence of the Resurrection, Palmer understood holiness to be the practice of abiding in the presence of God and yielding to the authority of God's word at all times. To borrow the language of von Hügel, Palmer saw this yieldedness not as the fearful surrender of slaves avoiding punishment, nor the self-seeking surrender of mercenaries who work for a reward, but a "pure" surrender of children to their Father, borne of pure love.[36] Moreover Palmer's understanding of "abiding in God" is thoroughly Trinitarian and Christocentric. She dwells in the Trinity and the Trinity dwells in her, empowering her to become increasingly holy as she is given increasing revelation of "the doctrine of Christ."[37]

Dark Night of the Soul

Among the most troubling and misunderstood aspects of apophatic mysticism is the phenomenon that has come to be called the dark night of the soul. John Wesley, after a protracted struggle to understand and accept the dark night during his early attraction to Christian mysticism, finally jettisoned the attempt because he could not simultaneously "feel

35. The many seasons in which Phoebe had to rely on "the naked Word of God alone" were for her, I believe, a part of the dark night of the soul, which she intermittently experienced for the rest of her life.

36. Von Hügel, 166; Oden, 187–90; Palmer, *Way of Holiness*, 20.

37. Palmer, *Way of Holiness*, 136–37.

assurance" and embrace what he understood to be the interminable "unknowing" of the night.[38] As discussed earlier, Wesley's disjuncture from Christian mysticism lasted for several decades primarily because of his repugnance toward the dark night. Thus the significance of the dark night in Palmer's life and thought is all the more ironic in the development of Wesleyan theology.

The dark night of the soul is often explained as part of the three-fold process of Christian spiritual transformation historically described as purgation, illumination and union. This threefold conceptual framework has origins in Scripture in the pattern of Christ's death and resurrection as found in Eph 4:11–24. In that passage Paul exhorts believers to die to the old self and "put on Christ," putting away all that is of the old life and its ego-driven concerns.

Patristic theologians beginning with Origen (185–254), and culminating in Evagrius Ponticus (346–399), laid the groundwork for the articulation of the three ways. Pseudo-Dionysius (ca. 500) labeled the three stages as purgation, illumination and union.[39] The concept of a threefold path for spiritual advancement received further, somewhat more lyrical explication at the hands of the mystics Bernard of Clairvaux (1090–1153) and Catherine of Siena (1347–1380). By the time of the Quietist controversy in the seventeenth century, "the three ways" had become so foundational to Roman Catholic spirituality that Miguel de Molinos, one of the proponents of Quietism, was pronounced a heretic partly because of his rejection of the three ways as a norm for spiritual advancement.[40]

Whether the three stages are successive phases or simultaneous and repeated forms of spiritual growth that characterize the spiritual journey, remains controversial. St. Teresa of Avila among others, believed the three ways to be successive stages. St. Bonaventure, on the other hand, saw a cyclical pattern in the three ways, which repeats itself

38. Tuttle, 106–7. Whether Wesley's understanding of the "unknowing" was correct according to the mystics' understanding is unclear. It could be argued that Wesley was seeking to accept negative or dark experiences as being definitive of mystical spirituality and finally gave up, exhausted. If that is the case, according to McIntosh and Turner's position, Wesley missed the point, for the point of apophatic mysticism is a relativization of experience in general, rather than an emphasis on negative or dark experiences.

39. McGonigle, "Three Ways," 963–65.

40. Ibid., 963.

again and again in the life of the believer. Some commentators argue the three ways are coexistent.[41]

As McGonigle highlights, the three ways are not to be understood as a rigid formula for spiritual development. They are, rather, self-recorded descriptions of the path which many mystics and saints walked on their own journeys toward oneness with the Divine.[42] The precise experience of purgation, illumination or union varies with each individual. So does the mysterious de-selfing of the dark night.

According to Underhill the dark night is a season of loss of equilibrium as the soul transitions from the Illuminative Way to the Unitive Way.[43] This season is marked by "utter blankness and stagnation, so far as mystical activity is concerned . . . it is of the essence of its miseries that the once-possessed power of orison or contemplation now seems wholly lost."[44]

As Underhill explains, the dark night is a time of profound suffering, which takes a different form in each person according to personality, faith tradition and life experiences. The sorrow of the night may be felt primarily in the emotions, the intellect, in moral rectitude or the sense of holiness, and in the sense of companionship with God.[45] For all forms there is a sense of spiritual stagnation, reversal or even death. The former affective experiences of God seem to be gone, or but a dim and painful memory. The soul finds no pleasure or joy in spiritual reading, prayer or any other spiritually nourishing pursuits that formerly gave satisfaction.

Many who have traversed the night record experiences of temptation to immorality, to cast their faith away, to doubt God's existence and undergo other temptations that are experienced not only as genuine temptation but also as deep grief to the soul. The very presence of "vulgar" temptations is a shocking affront to the souls who previously seemed to have advanced far beyond the realm of base temptations.[46] This exposure to multiple layers of loss, the feeling of God's absence,

41. Ibid., 964.
42. Ibid., 965.
43. Underhill, *Mysticism*, 381.
44. Ibid.
45. Ibid., 389–93.
46. Ibid., 389–95.

coarse temptation and other manifestations of the night collectively cause a negation and removal of reliance upon self. Carefully constructed ego-driven ascetical spirituality is particularly stripped of its self-reliance, causing the believer to have to trust in the sheer grace of God. Thus, Underhill reports, the various forms of the dark night lead to the same result: "The function of this episode of the Mystic Way is to cure the soul of the innate tendency to seek and rest in spiritual joys."[47]

In addition to St. John of the Cross and St. Teresa of Avila who are often studied as exemplars of the dark night, Underhill points to Madame Guyon as an "unparalleled study" for the phenomenon of the dark night. The oft-maligned seventeenth century French mystic, though considered far from an exemplary mystic by many Catholic commentators,[48] kept detailed records of her own experiences of the night and did not attempt to control the state of her soul. Guyon saw herself as "God's weathercock," and wrote accordingly.[49]

As noted earlier, in the development of Wesleyan holiness spirituality Guyon plays a special role. Her descriptions of the dark night, though not considered paradigmatic of Christian mysticism by many Catholic commentators, probably had more influence on Wesleyan holiness thought than did the writings of St. John of the Cross or St. Teresa of Avila. Wesley, who early in his career rejected Madame Guyon along with the other mystics, in the last years of his life praised her as one whose holiness would be hard to match over the course of many centuries.[50] Note again that Guyon is one of the eight mystics whose writing made it into Wesley's *Christian Library*.[51] The peculiar sufferings of the

47. Ibid., 395.

48. For example, in Livingstone, *The Concise Oxford Dictionary of the Christian Church*, 227–28, Guyon is labeled a Quietist.

49. Underhill, *Mysticism*, 384.

50. Orcibal, "Theological Originality," 94.

51. In addition to Wesley's *Christian Library*, several versions of Guyon's autobiography were printed by different holiness publishers at the time of Palmer's ministry, including one by Thomas Upham and another by the Salvation Army. William and Catherine Booth, who founded the Salvation Army, were disciples of Palmer and their ministry was in no small part borne out of Palmer's holiness teaching. One abridgement of Guyon's story published by the Salvation Army in 1885 describes Guyon as an exemplary holiness Christian, one who was "saved," "sanctified," and who "witnessed" to the monks about "sanctification." The dark night of the soul is described in this document through citations of Guyon's autobiography, but the editorial emphasis is placed upon sanctification and full salvation as the result of Guyon's embracing the night in

French woman in her dark night and her response to them, left a permanent mark in the heart of Wesley and many of his followers.

While some commentators argue that the dark night is simply an archaic way of explaining clinical depression, Denys Turner offers a persuasive argument against such a conclusion, drawing from St. John of the Cross who himself makes distinctions between "melancholia" and the dark night. According to Turner, the dark night is actually a "dialectical critique of experientialist tendencies."[52] Although both phenomena have similar symptoms, depression is caused by physiological reasons and upon its cure the sufferer resumes his or her previous state of being.[53] The dark night, however, is caused by a "superabundance of light," and upon the conclusion of a dark night the one who suffered has been transformed into greater holiness and freedom by the experience.[54] Turner's crisp distinction between the dark night and clinical depression skirts the reality of Underhill's observation that often the dark night is precipitated by experiences of loss. That is, sometimes depression is situational; it is not always induced by a chemical imbalance per se. Sometimes depression is a part of the dark night, as well, as is noted by Underhill and others. Turner is correct however in observing that the dark night is not simply another name for clinical depression. The two conditions may be related but they are not the same thing.

St. John of the Cross divides the dark night into four progressive states: active night of the senses, active night of the spirit, passive night of the senses and passive night of the spirit.[55] The cumulative effect of these four states is the deconstruction of self-centeredness in the mystic

---

trusting surrender to God's providence. While this abridgement was written by followers of Palmer after her death, thus it was not a direct endorsement of Guyon by Palmer, the concepts in it were linked with her theology. The authors use Palmer's language, in other words, to describe the experiences of Guyon. George R., *Madame Jeanne de la Mothe Guyon.* Typical of such publications at the time, the last name of the editor/annotator is not given.

52. Turner, *Darkness of God,* 227.

53. This is Turner's perspective. Depression is a complex phenomenon which involves body, mind and spirit. It can be situationally introduced such as in the case of grief, yet become a long-term physical, emotional and spiritual problem when seratonin levels are depleted. Spiritually the sufferer may experience the situational cause and physical effects of the depression as a form of spiritual abandonment.

54. Ibid., 235.

55. St. John of the Cross, *The Dark Night of the Soul.* http://www.ccel.org/j/john_cross/dark_night/dark_night.html.

and the exposure and removal of subtle idolatry in the mystic in terms of associating God with created things or viewing God as one more "thing." The dark night brings about the necessary detachment from created things so that the mystic may love all things in God rather than in and of themselves.

The "darkness" of the night is not because of God's absence, though it often feels like God is absent. Rather, the darkness is due to the soul's coming into contact with God's brilliance to such a degree that spiritual vision itself is blinded, at least temporarily.

As Turner explains, beginning with Pseudo Dionysius (for whom he prefers the older appellation, Denys the Areopagite), apophatic mysticism in Christian traditions is a Greek-Hebrew blend of Plato's "Allegory of the Cave" and the Old Testament account of Moses on Mt. Sinai receiving the Law.[56] In Plato's allegory the philosopher gains philosophical enlightenment by leaving the dark cave and going into the broad light of day. At first the daylight is painful and blinding. In time the philosopher's eyes adjust to the superabundance of light, allowing him to comprehend reality as never before. He returns to the cave to share with others the beauty of the real world over against the supposed reality of the cave-dwellers' shadow world. Turner explains that Pseudo Dionysius re-interpreted Plato's allegory as a narrative that describes the superabundance of light that is initially experienced as a "bright darkness" in Christian spiritual enlightenment. The paradigm for the painfully blinding brilliance of God is found first in the Old Testament in Moses' encounter with Yahweh on Mt. Sinai.[57] In the New Testament the brilliant darkness of God overwhelms Saul on the road to Damascus when he encounters the risen Lord.[58]

According to Turner, the active night of the spirit is a time in which ascetical practices are used by the mystic as a means to draw closer to God and become more holy. The last phase of the dark night, however, the passive night of the spirit, is a God-initiated period of time in which the mystic's self-driven asceticism undergoes deconstruction. The individual realizes that no matter how much he or she does to purify him or herself, in the final analysis only God can bring about such purity. There

56. Turner, *Darkness of God*, 13–18.

57. Exod 33–34.

58. Acts 9.

is a certain "paralysis of agency" that is characteristic of this season of purgative dryness, argues Turner, that is also marked by the individual's pain at not being able to serve God through the former asceticism. This pain is one of the features that distinguish the dark night from clinical depression.[59]

Although the individual who is experiencing the night cannot tell what God is doing or how God is doing it, for the whole encounter is fraught with "unknowing," the grace and excess of light which are causing the darkness are experienced as deprivation. The pain is a pain of deprivation and loss.[60] For many people the felt experience is one of God-forsakenness, or that God and all former experiences of God are no longer "real."

A very small list of those who have recorded dark night experiences include Henry Suso, Johann Tauler, Rulman Merswin, Angela of Foligno, Madame Guyon, Mechthild of Magdeburg, St. Teresa of Avila, St. John of the Cross, George Fox, Thomas R. Kelly, and Phoebe Palmer. While Palmer did not label her experiences a "dark night of the soul" the descriptions of her experiences parallel those of other mystics who suffered the peculiar "trials and crosses" of the night.

Palmer details numerous episodes in her life in which she suffered precisely the kinds of sufferings described by other mystics in the dark night. The following are but two examples. The first comes from *The Way of Holiness* and is a general description of these repeated sufferings:

> These trials, though they sometimes arose from outward causes, were generally inward and the struggle they caused is indescribable; in the midst of which she was often called to lean so entirely, "with *naked* promise," that nature was sometimes tempted in its shrinkings to say, "My God, why has thou forsaken me?" but still holding with an unyielding grasp upon the promise, "I will never leave nor forsake thee." And believing that the Saviour was treading "the wine press *alone*, and of the people there was none with him," when he gave utterance to this expression, she was checked ere she had given words to the thought, and instead of indulging in those words, which none but He who "wept that man might smile," *need* use, she said in the language of faith, "My God, thou hast not forsaken me."[61]

59. Turner, *Darkness of God*, 237, 242.

60. Ibid.

61. Palmer, *Way of Holiness*, 66.

The next excerpt is from the call vision Palmer recorded shortly before her death, the defining vision she had not felt free to write about prior to that time though it occurred thirty-four years earlier. The title she gave to this document was "Refining Processes." Note in particular the crushing awe and profound humiliation Palmer describes as she encounters the living God, the temptations to think God had forsaken her, the negation of ego and the stripping away of reliance upon previous spiritual experiences:

> The peculiar experience of which I am about to speak occurred August 1840, was preceded by humiliations of soul that I can scarcely attempt to describe. I am sure I know what David meant when he exclaimed "I am a worm and no man." I knew, and *felt* that I was shielded by the atonement, and therefore there was no condemnation, but the *Word of the Lord* was intensified, in a manner that human language cannot portray. For days, and nights in succession it penetrated my soul, as if it would part it asunder "sharper than any two-edged sword, piercing even to the dividing of soul, and spirit, and of the joints and marrow, and as a discerner of the thoughts and intents of the heart." My naked soul seemed to be tending as in the more immediate presence of the All-seeing, to whom all things are naked and open. Such piercing views of my utter nothingness, and the intense spirituality of the *Word of God,* seemingly would have crushed me, but I pleaded that my spirit might not fail before Him. In a sense beyond any former experiences I could say "I have heard of thee by the hearing of the ear; but now mine eye seeth thee, wherefore I abhor myself in dust and ashes."
>
> Previous to this deep realization of the sharpness of the two-edged sword, my experience had generally been joyous. Though I had not been without oft repeated conflicts, conquest had so quickly succeeded each conflict, that the joy of victory was ever in my heart, and on my lips. For many days in succession all sensible, joyous experiences were withheld, and I was shut up to the exercise of "naked faith in a naked promise." The cruel tempter said, that the Lord whom I loved supremely, had forsaken me, that I had surely in some unknown way offended. But I kept hold of the promise, "If in any thing ye be otherwise minded, God will reveal even this to you." And as God in answer to special and importunate prayer did not reveal anything, I still held strongly the shield of faith, saying sooner will I die than doubt. Often amid this great trial of my faith, did the providences of God seem to contradict the promises. Yet knowing that the ways

of God are all perfect, I knew that in the end he would bring order out of apparent confusion.[62]

On her "Day of Days" in July 1837, when Palmer made her Altar Covenant, one of the eight temptations with which she struggled was the fear that she might never receive spiritual consolations or "manifestations" for the rest of her life. In other words, she had to decide to walk by faith even if it meant remaining in a permanent state of unknowing or the dark night:

> Still the enemy withstood me, with the suggestion, "Suppose you should be called to live a long life, till you are three score or a hundred years old, and never have any of those manifestations that others enjoy—never have anything but the naked Word of God upon which to rely; and should die, and come up before your Judge, without ever having had anything but the naked Word to assure your faith?"[63]

Palmer refuted the temptation by stating that she was indeed willing to spend the rest of her life in a state of apophatic trust, walking by faith instead of sight, citing the story of Abraham's call in which: "by *faith* he journeyed, not knowing whither he went."[64]

Even after making this commitment Palmer reports that the adversary taunted her, for no "manifestation," emotional or otherwise, happened after she made the Altar Covenant. Palmer simply writes that she was "shut up to faith—*naked faith in a naked promise.*"[65]

The Theological Impact of Apophatic Mysticism

Palmer's apophatic mysticism was foundational to her self-understanding, her sense of call to ministry, the kinds of sacrifices she would be willing to make in order to answer that call, and not least, the content of her theology. There are at least four ways in which apophatic mysticism helped to shape her theology. Each of these elements must be grasped in order to properly understand her sanctification theology, yet each of them has been distorted by later interpreters of her teaching, particu-

---

62. Oden, *Selected Writings*, 322.
63. Wheatley, *Life and Letters*, 41.
64. Ibid.
65. Ibid., 42.

larly in the concepts of works-righteousness and instantaneous sinless perfection.

First and foremost, Palmer experientially came to understand that sanctification cannot come about through good works, devotional exercises, emotional "enthusiasm" or any other self-energized effort. Like justification, sanctification is the gift of God, given by grace. Even the desire to become holy is a gift of grace, Palmer argued. In a letter of spiritual direction to a woman who guiltily confessed she did not desire holiness, Palmer counseled: "But you cannot work a willingness in yourself. It is only Christ that can work in you that which is well-pleasing in his sight; but how can He do it, until you yield yourself wholly up to him?"[66] The solution was for the woman to ask Christ to make her heart willing. By offering up herself as she was, including her unwilling heart, she could open herself to receive the transforming grace of Christ.

To another "worldling" Palmer offered comfort, saying there was no need to fear surrendering all to Jesus, since he would "bear her, cross and all, if she would only resolve in his strength to take it up."[67] Works of righteousness are the after-effect of being surrendered to Christ, and can only take place because of grace resident within the soul of the believer.[68] Although holiness of lifestyle should be expected of those who have been sanctified, it is clearly an outcome and not the cause of sanctification.

Despite the clarity of these teachings in Palmer's writings, some later interpreters who missed the apophatic element of Palmer's thought have presented her in an entirely different light. For example Theodore Hovet proposes that Palmer's altar theology is, in essence, a self-centered and self-motivated program for personal transformation:

> Significantly, however, she saw the spiritual experience [of sanctification] as the result of the actions she herself had taken to overcome spiritual darkness rather than as a miraculous gift of a compassionate God. She was convinced that by ignoring the "opinions and experience of professors" in the church on the nature of spiritual rebirth and instead taking "the blessed word more closely to the companionship of [her] heart" she had discovered a "practical" way by which the individual "alone and

66. Palmer, *Full Salvation*, 51–52.

67. Ibid.

68. Ibid., 52.

unaided," as one of her followers put it, could spiritually trans-
form herself.[69]

Hovet goes on to claim that Palmer's altar phraseology was a
"pragmatic modification" of the classical mystical way of purgation, and
goes so far as to say that "the altar phraseology described a process of
self-creation." It is a self-creation, Hovet declares, that Palmer believes is
done by human effort "without a baptism of the spirit."[70] According to
Hovet, then, Palmer teaches a works righteousness, or behavior oriented
form of holiness that is generated not just within oneself but *by* oneself.
One wonders how Hovet misses Palmer's repeated and most basic assertion that "the altar sanctifies the gift" and "Christ is the altar." While
Hovet's claim seems unlikely in light of Palmer's own words, works
righteousness came to be associated with Palmer in several Holiness
denominations that were founded by Palmer's disciples. Palmer's experience of grace in the midst of apophatic surrender was lost in such
interpretations.

The second influence of Palmer's mystical experience is seen in
her understanding of sanctification as both an instantaneous work—a
promise to be believed—and a process to be lived. According to Palmer
there is no "fixity" to sanctification, and she seems ambiguous about a
removal of the root of original sin, as historically taught by the Church
of the Nazarene, the largest of the Holiness denominations that grew
out of Palmer's teaching.[71] Using the example of a child learning to
read, Palmer explains that souls entering into the way of holiness are
like children who have mastered the alphabet. It is true that they can
"read," but their ability to read and the depth with which they read will
be a life-long process of growth, one which is never finished. In the
same way, sanctified believers are to continuously "go on to perfection,"
(or "completion"), never ceasing to grow more holy in this lifetime. It
is possible for believers to choose to stop going on to holiness and to

69. Hovet, "Phoebe Palmer's 'Altar Phraseology,'" 265. One wonders what Hovet
does with Palmer's repeated emphasis on the necessity of the "full baptism of the Holy
Ghost," which is sanctification. Palmer, *Promise of the Father*, 252, 257–58. Also see
White, *Beauty of Holiness*, 126–28 for a discussion of Palmer's use of Pentecostal language to describe sanctification.

70. Ibid., 268–69.

71. Raser, "Church of the Nazarene"; M.D. Strege, "Sanctification" in Reid, Linder, et
al., *Dictionary of Christianity in America*, 274–75; 1045–46.

choose to abandon faith, for the capacity for sin ever remains in the believer in this lifetime.

If the possibility of sin could be removed at the moment of sanctification there would be no need for concern about Satan, Palmer argues. Yet the Bible clearly teaches *saints* to be alert, mindful of Satan's schemes. "How deceived is he who imagines that he has attained a higher state, where the life of nature is so extinct that Satan can find no ground to work upon—a state of boasted exemption from his attacks!"[72] Indeed, the idea of sinless perfection is one of the "refined mysticisms" Palmer attacks in the later thought of Thomas Upham.[73]

According to Palmer, no believer is ever beyond the pale of temptation. Temptation always taps into an inner weakness, requiring the believer to cast self upon God's mercy at all times, both for discernment to recognize Satan's wiles, and for the strength to resist.[74] The key to progressive growth in holiness is not a one-time experience of surrender. The key is a moment-by-moment placing of the self on the altar of Jesus, or in Brother Lawrence's words, the practice of the presence of God:

> It is only by an entire and continual reliance on Christ, that a state of entire sanctification can be retained. The sacrifices under the old dispensation were sanctified by the altar upon which they were laid. Had the offerer resumed the sacrifice, to the degree he resumed it, to that degree it would have ceased to be sanctified; for it was the *altar* that sanctified the gift.[75]

Although Palmer claimed to have walked continuously in the presence of God for more than eighteen years, thus remaining on the altar of Christ, she attributed each moment of her consecration to the sheer grace of God.[76]

The third major element of Palmer's sanctification theology that grew directly from her apophatic mysticism is her emphasis on heart-purity as empowerment for ministry. Reminiscent of Kierkegaard's phrase, "purity of heart is to will one thing," Palmer sees purity of heart

72. Ibid., 148–49.

73. Salter, "Mysticism in American Wesleyanism: Thomas Upham," 102.

74. Ibid., 152–55.

75. Oden, *Selected Writings*, 200.

76. Palmer, *Full Salvation*, 175.

as the one-ing of the believer's will with God's will, and she understands that God's will above all else is to reach lost souls.[77] The inevitable outcome of sanctification is the unleashing of the power of God in one's life to do the "impossible," particularly in the realm of fruitful ministry.[78]

As we have seen, in her own life Palmer experienced the call to ministry and the power to answer that call as a result of her experience of mystical surrender. Though she could not know immediately just how much that call would require of her, from the beginning she had a sense that her experience of "resting in the Word of God" was preparing her to be a channel of God's redeeming love for thousands. "We know that Christ has purchased for us all the grace we need, but we do not properly appreciate the fact that our privileges are high responsibilities—solemn duties," writes Palmer concerning the graced experience of heart purity.[79] The experience of Spirit baptism is described as a responsibility given so that God can be made known to the world.

Thus heart purity with its apophatic purgation and subsequent unification of the believer's will with God's will, is neither a privatized spiritual experience nor is it concerned chiefly with acts of individual piety. Rather, heart purity is the result of the baptism of the Holy Spirit, a gift of power given to the Church so that God's will might be done, meaning that souls might be won to Christ.

The fourth major influence of Palmer's apophatic mysticism on her theology is her emphasis on the difference between faith and feeling. "Remember," Palmer admonishes, "the just shall live by faith," not ecstasies. Holiness is the state of being in which all the powers of soul and body are consciously given up to God."[80] Faith is neither emotion nor asceticism. Rather, faith is "naked trust in the naked Word of God." "One act of faith can raise the dead to life, and can do more for us than twenty years of groans and tears without it,"[81] writes Palmer, who knows first-hand what it means to experience both mystical ecstasy and the dark night of the soul. While emotions are not the definitive proof of having received sanctification, emotions are not to be despised. Palmer

77. This is actually the title of one of Kierkegaard's books. Kierkegaard, *Purity of Heart Is to Will One Thing.*

78. Oden, *Selected Writings*, 264; Palmer, *Full Salvation*, 55.

79. Palmer, *Full Salvation*, 75.

80. Oden, *Selected Writings*, 197.

81. Palmer, *Full Salvation*, 106.

describes many personal experiences of passionate, enraptured worship and moments of kataphatic mystical union. But her focus is always on the God whose word is true, not on the emotions she feels.

Conclusion

What so many Wesleyan commentators have missed about Palmer's altar theology is precisely this: her fundamental apophatic mysticism, arising from her own journey as a mystic. In the next chapter we will consider Palmer's distinctly Wesleyan, apophatic altar theology.

4

Altar Theology and the Shorter Way

AS MENTIONED ELSEWHERE, THE SHORTER WAY INVOLVES THREE STEPS, each of which has its own assumptions about Scripture, faith and the nature of salvation. These steps are entire consecration, faith, and testimony. Palmer's three steps may be understood as events that take place both at the beginning of sanctification, as literal steps, and also as a simultaneous three-fold process that is to characterize the journey of a sanctified believer for the rest of his or her life. Because of the latter meaning, the labeling of these three elements of Palmer's altar theology as "steps" has in some ways contributed to skewed interpretations of the shorter way.

Palmer understands human holiness to be the experience of entire devotion to God, of being a living sacrifice on the altar of Christ, of being continuously "washed, cleansed, and renewed after the image of God" as one is ceaselessly presented to God.[1] Romans 12:1–2 is a critical text for Palmer and as such, illustrates her affirmation of the process of sanctification:

> I beseech you therefore, brethren, by the mercies of God, that ye present your bodies a living sacrifice, holy, acceptable unto God, which is your reasonable service. And be not conformed to this world: but be ye transformed by the renewing of your mind, that ye may prove what is that good, and acceptable, and perfect will of God.[2]

The Apostle's phrase "living sacrifice" implies a dynamic, ongoing, organic process involving daily choice. Living sacrifices must choose

---

1. Excerpted in Oden, *Selected Writings*, 189. The text is originally from Palmer, *Entire Devotion to God*, section II.

2. Rom 12:1–2, Authorized Version.

daily whether to "stay on the altar." The transformation that is expected of sanctified believers is a journey that takes time as the mind is gradually and increasingly "renewed." Sanctification is a "way" of holiness, writes Palmer, another image that implies movement, process, time, growth, and journey.[3] The very language of Scripture is both/and in terms of sanctification as an event and a process. Hebrews, the biblical book with Palmer's premier texts on holiness, applies a typological hermeneutic to the Exodus event to teach Christians that one cannot simply enter the promised land, one must increasingly "possess" it through ongoing obedience to God.

Palmer's use of the term "shorter way" does not then imply absence of process or journey. Nor does the phrase necessarily imply instantaneousness over process. Rather, the word "shorter" underscores the potential for entering the way of holiness sooner rather than later, and gives a method for entering the way of holiness.[4] For Palmer, sanctification is the beginning, not the end of the journey of holiness.[5] The sooner one enters the way of holiness the sooner one will be empowered for lifelong service and purity of heart, with which to love God and neighbor.

Palmer cites numerous texts from both Old Testament and New Testament in which God's people are commanded to be holy or be sanctified.[6] Of these texts, Heb 12:14 is most prominent: "Follow peace with all men, and holiness, without which no man will see the Lord." Other commands to holiness include Lev 11:45, "I am the Lord who brought

3. This phrase appears many times in Palmer's writing and is the title of her most popular book.

4. St. Thérèse of Lisieux (1873–1897), the French Carmelite sister whose spiritual autobiography quickly became a spiritual classic after her untimely death, offers strikingly similar prayer and imagery in her "Act of Oblation to Merciful Love" and in her description of having discovered a way to holiness that is "little, very straight, very short, and totally new." It is also noteworthy that when describing how God speaks to her to show her the short way, St. Thérèse calls the Bible the "mouth of Eternal Wisdom. Here her language is much like Palmer's, who understood Scripture to be the voice of the Holy Spirit. St. Thérèse of Lisieux, *Story of a Soul*, 207–8, 276–77.

5. Recall that putting sanctification at the beginning rather than the end of the Christian journey is a shift in emphasis that is attributed to Palmer, but originating in Fletcher. White, "Phoebe Palmer and the Development of Pentecostal Pneumatology," 198–99.

6. Excerpted in Oden, *Selected Writings*, 189. The text is originally from Palmer, *Entire Devotion to God*, section II.

you up out of Egypt to be your God; therefore be holy, because I am holy," and 2 Cor 7:1, "Since we have these promises, dear friends, let us purify ourselves from everything that contaminates body and spirit, perfecting holiness out of reverence for God." These passages when taken in context also imply the importance of daily choice in remaining in the way of holiness.

At times Palmer seems to go so far as to give the impression that a professing Christian could actually miss out on heaven if he or she has not entered the way of holiness, since "without holiness, no man will see the Lord."[7] In this respect she seems to edge toward Pelagianism, and it is this element of her altar theology that may have partially contributed to a works righteousness tendency in later holiness theology.[8] At the same time it must be said that Palmer's emphasis on grace as the divine energy that makes holiness possible, serves to balance her occasional semi-Pelagian statements.

The only way for a sanctified believer to stay holy, according to Palmer, is to keep everything "on the altar." For in Palmer's altar theology it is the altar that sanctifies the gift. (Note again the relationship between grace and human cooperation with the Holy Spirit.) True to her Wesleyan, Arminian theological heritage, she believes that the Christian never loses his or her free will, with which continuous decisions are made about keeping on or removing from the altar, that which has previously been consecrated. The warning passages of Heb 4:1–11, 6:4–6, 10:26–39, and 12:14–29 carry somber messages of judgment for those who have once walked in the way of holiness, then lost their way through disobedience. Putting all on the altar is an ongoing choice with serious ramifications.

Though many of Palmer's theological progeny have focused on the instantaneous side of the shorter way (having a personal "day of days," so to speak, to which one could point as the day of one's sanctification), it is already evident from the brief citations of her own descriptions of

---

7. Both White and Dieter are in agreement that although Palmer does not explicitly say people will go to hell if they are not sanctified, her teaching generally leaves this impression. In this regard Palmer's holiness emphasis, while correcting what she perceived to be a lukewarm climate in the church, could be stretched to an extreme beyond her original intent. White, *The Beauty of Holiness*, 133–34.

8. The biggest factors leading to works righteousness in the later holiness movement are detailed in chapter 5.

the shorter way that a daily process of kenosis is involved, one which requires all three "steps" on an ongoing basis.[9] Palmer issues repeated admonitions against losing one's holiness, and the need to walk faithfully day by day in order to retain a state of sanctification:

> It is only by an entire and continual reliance on Christ, that a state of entire sanctification can be retained. The sacrifices under the old dispensation were sanctified by the altar upon which they were laid. Had the offerer resumed the sacrifice, to the degree he resumed it, to that degree it would have ceased to be sanctified; for it was the *altar* that sanctified the gift.[10]

Despite Palmer's teaching on the ongoing process of being made holy, this side of her teaching was subsequently minimized, while the three-step, shorter way was emphasized as an instantaneous event by those who followed her.

Palmer's "altar theology," the foundation of her shorter way of sanctification, centers on two concepts: first that the altar sanctifies the gift, and second that Christ himself is the altar. As always, these convictions are based upon Scripture. Palmer's understanding that the altar sanctifies the gift is based upon texts from Exodus and Matthew, among others:

> The altar, thus provided by the conjoint testimony of the Father, Son and Holy Spirit, is Christ. His sacrificial death and sufferings are the sinner's plea; the immutable promises of the Lord Jehovah the ground of claim. If true to the Spirit's operations on the heart, men, as workers together with God, confess their sins, the faithfulness and justice of God stand pledged not only to *forgive*, but also to *cleanse from all unrighteousness*.
>
> By the resolve to be a "Bible Christian," this traveler in the "way of holiness" placed herself in the way to receive the direct teachings of the Spirit, and in the *one* and the only *way* for the attainment of salvation promised in the gospel of Christ, inasmuch as it is written, "He became the author of eternal salvation to all them that *obey him*.
>
> And by the determination to consecrate all upon the altar of sacrifice to God, with the resolve to "enter into the bonds of

---

9. For more on the reification of the instantaneous side of the shorter way see Truesdale, "The Reification of Sanctification."

10. Excerpted in Oden, *Selected Writings*, 200. Originally found in Palmer, *Entire Devotion to God*, section XVI.

an everlasting covenant to be wholly the Lord's for time and eternity," and then acting in conformity with this decision *actually laying all upon the altar*, by the most unequivocal Scripture testimony, she laid herself under the most solemn obligation *to believe that the sacrifice became the Lord's property; and by virtue of the altar upon which the offering was laid, became "holy" and "acceptable."*

The written testimony of the Old and New Testament Scriptures upon which, to her mind, the obligation for this belief rested, was brought out by comparing the design, and bearing of the old and new covenant dispensations, thus: the old ordained that an altar be erected. See Exodus 27:1, etc. This altar, before being eligible for the reception of offerings, was to be "atoned for," cleansed and sanctified. See Exodus 29:36–37. This being done, it was ordained by God to be "an altar most holy, whatsoever toucheth the altar shall be holy." Being thus proclaimed by the fiat of the Holy One "an altar most holy," whatever *touched* the altar became holy, virtually the Lord's *property, sanctified to his service.* The sacredness and perpetuity of this ordinance were recognized by "God manifest in the flesh," centuries afterward. "The *altar* that sanctifieth the gift." See Matthew 23:19.[11]

Palmer's citations from Exodus 29 are part of a lengthy section giving instructions for the consecration of priests. The quote is thus doubly significant in that Palmer's theological thrust in sanctification is toward preparedness of the church for holy, priestly service in the world.[12] Not only is she making a statement about the altar sanctifying the gift, she is subtly reinforcing one of her primary themes in sanctification, which is empowerment for holy service. The promise of the Father is given so that the gospel may be proclaimed everywhere, not just through professional clergy, but through every Spirit-baptized son and daughter of God. Sanctification is much more concerned with taking the Gospel to "Jerusalem, Judea, Samaria, and the uttermost parts of the earth"[13] than with individual piety or asceticism.

Throughout the cultus regulations of Exodus 29 the emphasis is on the "set-apartness" of holiness. Whatever is sanctified or consecrated is completely set apart for God. The many offerings, cleansing rituals, priestly garments, anointing procedures and explicit times for each

11. Palmer, *Way of Holiness*, 43–44.

12. For the biblical concept of the priesthood of all believers see 1 Pet 2:9–10.

13. Acts 1:8.

ritual detailed in Exodus 29 are all meant to underscore the solemnity of the covenant. Once consecrated, the priests will belong wholly to God. They will no longer be like other Israelites and will not live according to other tribes' standards.

The "otherness" of the Levites is especially pronounced in the prohibition against their owning land. According to Num 18:20–21 the only inheritance the Levites will have is the tithe of the rest of the Israelites. The Levites are to understand that they are not their own but are actually God's gift to the rest of the Israelites, to prevent God's wrath from having to be released on the other Israelites.[14] The consecrated priests are to mediate God's presence to the rest of Israel. (Israel, in turn, is to mediate God's presence to the whole world.) That holy task is to become their singular, guiding vision. They do not have other options that are acceptable to God. Several times in Numbers 18 the Levites are warned that no one but properly consecrated priests are to care for the Tent of Testimony. Any ordinary person who attempts to go near the sanctuary or altar will die.

Similar expectations are placed upon sanctified believers who have placed all upon the altar of Christ. Once sanctified, they will be "the Lord's *property*," writes Palmer. Unlike other people who might cling to material wealth, status and other accoutrements of success, sanctified Christians are on a journey of holiness, their lives utterly given over to God's purposes. The testimony of those who are sanctified becomes the contemporary version of taking the Gospel to "Jerusalem, Judea, Samaria, and the uttermost parts of the earth." Sanctified believers are the priestly mediators of God's saving love to a world in desperate need.

Those who are sanctified cannot claim holiness based upon personal effort. As Palmer stresses so often, it is the altar that sanctifies the gift. At the center of Exodus 29 and its various rites of consecration is the altar upon which the offerings are made. Before the priests could be consecrated the altar itself had to first be sanctified. Once the altar was "atoned for," (that is cleansed and set apart exclusively for God according to Exod 29:37), it became holy therefore anything that touched it was also made holy. The gifts offered there were not intrinsically holy rather the altar of sacrifice was what sanctified the gifts.

14. Num 18:5–6.

Under the new covenant, argues Palmer, Christ is the altar. "The altar, thus provided by the conjoint testimony of the Father, Son, and Holy Spirit, is Christ. His sacrificial death and sufferings are the sinner's plea; the immutable promises of the Lord Jehovah the ground of claim."[15]

Palmer's understanding of Christ as the altar is based upon an interpretation of Heb 13:10 in which believers are assured: "We have an altar from which those who officiate in the tent have no right to eat." Following Adam Clarke and others, Palmer understands the altar in this passage and the rest of Hebrews to be Christ. In Hebrews Christ is all three: the sacrifice, the priest and the altar. This interpretation is consistent not only with Clarke, but also with much of Church tradition since antiquity.[16]

In citing Jesus as the altar according to Heb 13:10, by extension Palmer also refers to the subsequent instructions for those who would place themselves on the altar. Sanctified believers, following the instructions of verses 13–16, express their sanctification in several ways. First they are willing to bear whatever disgrace or persecution the world might heap upon them, for they are identified with Jesus' interests "outside the camp" (Heb 13:13). The desire for human approval, in other words, no longer has power over the sanctified Christian. Moreover, the set apart ones are on pilgrimage, detached from this world and its seductions (verse 14). The true destination, the true home lies ahead in eternity. Therefore the sanctified are in this world as sojourners rather than citizens. The sacrifices that are to be offered by the priestly, sanctified believers are living sacrifices of praise, and lips confessing the name of Jesus (verse 15).

Palmer's sanctification theology is deeply rooted in both Old and New Testaments, with special attention to passages having to do with priestly consecration, the role of Jesus as the altar, and the expectations of those who would walk in the way of holiness.

---

15. Palmer, *Way of Holiness*, 43. This is but one of numerous places in which this claim is made.

16. Again, note that contemporary NT scholars including Attridge and Lane are in agreement with Palmer's exegesis of the altar in Hebrews. "Altar" in Heb 13:10 is a metonymy for sacrifice, according to Lane, with Christ being the perfect and final sacrifice. See Lane, *Hebrews 9–13*, vol. 48, 538–39. Also see Attridge, *Hebrews*, 391.

Olah: The Whole Offering

Understanding, then, the foundation of her altar theology, let us consider the three parts of the shorter way of sanctification. The first step of the shorter way is the step of entire consecration, in which the individual takes inventory of every part of his or her life, willfully and with irrevocable commitment placing everything on the "altar" which is Christ himself. Nothing is held back. Romans 12:1–2, in which Paul exhorts believers to present themselves as living sacrifices is the scriptural command for this step. As part of this step the believer also implores God to reveal if there is anything that has not been surrendered. If anything is held back, whether it is a relationship, possessions, or even the sin of doubt, one cannot expect to receive the full blessing of sanctification.[17] The first step of the shorter way, then, is apophatic, a profound emptying of oneself onto the altar of Christ.

For Palmer, this kenotic prayer has the nature of a legal document such as a last will and testament. In her book *Entire Devotion to God* Palmer includes a representative covenant prayer that can be personalized.[18] Palmer's covenantal approach is consonant with the biblical commandments for preparing and giving to God the *olah*, the whole burnt offering. Palmer's preference for the theological model of Leviticus is in keeping with Jesus and the early church in their understanding of the meaning of Jesus' sacrificial death.[19] To more deeply plumb Palmer's intent in using the sacrificial language and image of *olah* to explain sanctification, let us return to Leviticus.

While Leviticus treats of both God's and humanity's actions in sanctification, clearly teaching that only God can sanctify people, the emphasis of the book lies in humanity's part in making things holy.[20] Together with M. Douglas, Wenham describes Levitical concepts of holiness as being as much about completeness and wholeness as about correct moral choices.[21] Old Testament laws forbidding the interbreeding of animals, mixing of different crops in the field and so on are symbolic

---

17. White, *Beauty of Holiness*, 136–37.

18. Ibid., 247.

19. Wenham, *Book of Leviticus*, 36–37.

20. Ibid., 22–23.

21. Ibid., 24.

of the core value of wholeness, completeness, and purity.[22] At the deepest level these laws and concepts of holiness all signify the importance of God's people avoiding syncretism. Throughout the prohibitions and commandments of Leviticus rings the refrain: "I am the Lord." There is only one God, Yahweh. His people are to belong utterly to him. Human holiness is about complete surrender of self to God, more than anything else.

God's holiness is intrinsic to God's being, and is not particularly about God's morality. Beyond God's judgment of sin there is little in the Pentateuch that defines God's holiness in terms of morality. The commandment to "be holy, for I am holy" is therefore a commandment to be fully set aside for God's purposes, to be whole and complete, to obey the law and to be one who does not profane the name of the Lord.

These kinds of expectations are all found in Palmer's understanding of holiness. The sanctified believer is one who is fully set aside for God's purposes, one who lives according to God's word in the Bible, one who does not profane the name of the Lord, and one who is made complete in Christ. Romans 12:1–2 describes this person as a living sacrifice, referring to the *olah*, the whole burnt offering of Leviticus 18.

The first requirement for a whole offering in Leviticus 18 is that the offering be ritually clean, for only clean animals can become holy. As Wenham notes, cleanness is more than purity, it "approximates to our notion of normality."[23] Specific kinds of animals are designated as acceptable for the whole offering: sheep, goats, cattle and birds. In order to qualify for the whole offering these animals have to be without blemish. One of Malachi's indictments against Israel was their "contemptible" practice of profaning God's name in using diseased, crippled and blind animals for the whole offering.[24]

The Old Testament requirement of sacrificial animals that were "clean" and "without blemish" takes on a new meaning in light of the New Testament. In Palmer's Wesleyan theology the believer who seeks sanctification is already justified. He or she, in other words, has already been made "clean" by the grace of justification. Imputed cleanness has made the person a candidate for becoming a living sacrifice, a whole of-

22. See Leviticus 19, for example.
23. Wenham, *Book of Leviticus*, 20.
24. Mal 1:7–8.

fering on the altar of Christ. The second work of grace, sanctification, is the imparted grace, which will make the person holy. Thus the justified believer is the "clean" and acceptable candidate for a living sacrifice.

The most distinguishing feature of the whole offering was that the entire animal except its skin (or crop if a bird) was burned on the altar.[25] Unlike other offerings, none of the whole offering was given to the priests. Wenham observes, "In the overfed West we can easily fail to realize what was involved in offering an unblemished animal in sacrifice. Meat was a rare luxury in OT times for all but the very rich (cf. Nathan's parable, 2 Sam 12:1–6). Yet even we might blanch if we saw a whole lamb or bull go up in smoke as a burnt offering. How much greater pangs must a poor Israelite have felt.[26]

The costliness of the sacrifice underscores the costliness of sin, for the whole offering was given to atone for human sin.[27] The purification offering described in Leviticus 4 and the guilt offering in Leviticus 5 are also designated to atone for sin, but the whole offering atones for sin in a somewhat different way.[28] The whole offering makes fellowship between God and humanity possible again after sin has caused a separation. The restoration of relationship provided by the burnt offering is suggested in Lev 14:20 and 16:24, as well as numerous other passages in the Old Testament.

The whole offering meant more than atonement for sin, however. It was also at times an act of worship, obedience, faith, or thanksgiving for deliverance.[29] In addition to these applications, the whole offering may be understood as a "ransom" paid by the worshipper.

Wenham offers a persuasive argument for ransom as the premier meaning of atonement in Lev 17:11, in which Yahweh says: "I have given the blood to make atonement for your lives, for the blood makes atonement at the price of a life."[30] This is the dominant meaning of all whole offerings, according to Wenham: "God in his mercy allowed sinful man

---

25. Lev 1:8, 16.

26. Wenham, *Book of Leviticus*, 51.

27. Lev 1:4.

28. Ibid., 57.

29. See Exod 18:11–12; 24:3–8, Num 6:14; 15:3, Ps 50; 66:13–15.

30. Wenham, *Book of Leviticus*, 60–61.

to offer a ransom payment for sins, so that he escaped the death penalty that his iniquities merit."[31]

The ransom aspect of the whole offering is especially evident in the instructions for the worshipper to lay hands upon or lean on the animal during the prayer. The laying on of hands coupled with sincere prayer from the heart are the human actions that make the sacrifice acceptable.[32]

How does all of this translate into Palmer's sanctification theology? There is no question that Palmer sees Christ as the ultimate sacrifice for sin. The atonement and ransom aspects of the whole offering apply to Christ, not to those seeking salvation and sanctification. That is, Christ is the perfect sacrifice once and for all. Christ has atoned for the sins of the world. Christ has ransomed the world, paying a debt the sinful world could not pay.[33] Palmer has a clear and unambiguous grasp on the reality of salvation by grace and not by works. Thus the atonement aspect of the whole offering is not what she has in mind in equating the whole offering with putting oneself on the altar.

According to Rom 12:1, Christians are to offer themselves as whole (albeit living) offerings as a grateful and reasonable response to God's mercy. Worship is the motivating factor for those who would truly seek sanctification. This is quite in keeping with the whole offering of the Old Testament as an act of worship, obedience, faith, and thanksgiving for deliverance from sin. The costliness of the whole offering also figures into Palmer's theology, in her insistence that the seeker put *all* on the altar.

From a standpoint of Palmer's apophatic spirituality, giving oneself as a whole offering is a supremely "negating" act of worship. The one who is on the altar is there utterly for God. No longer having a self-life apart from God, no longer having a will of his or her own, the Palmerian *olah* is one whose life is continuously ascending to God in the fire of kenotic adoration.[34] To make the choice daily, even hourly, to

31. Ibid., 61.

32. Lev 1:4; 3:2, 8, 13; 4:4, 15, 24; 16:21.

33. Palmer accepts a substitutionary model of atonement, as did Wesley, although with Wesley there are also therapeutic aspects to the atonement.

34. The Hebrew word for whole offering is of uncertain etymology, but many scholars believe it is related to the word for "ascending," with the smoke of the whole offering ascending as a pleasing aroma to God. Averbeck, "Olah," 406.

keep all on the altar, is an ongoing expression of apophatic spirituality. Just as in Leviticus the fragrance of the *olah* was a "soothing aroma" to God, the "aroma" of the living whole offering is a sweet and most precious fragrance to God.[35]

Faith in God's Promise

The second step of the shorter way is the exercise of faith: willfully trusting the promise of God in Scripture concerning sanctification, regardless of outward signs, emotions, or religious manifestations. This step requires "naked faith in the naked word of God," another form of apophasia.

Before considering what Palmer does mean by "naked faith" in this context, it must be emphasized that Palmer does not mean "faith that does not express itself in action." Palmer expects a holy lifestyle ultimately to manifest itself in those who claim to be sanctified.[36] Even though one might claim to be sanctified upon making a full surrender to God, prior to having had time to see the fruit of sanctification, Palmer expects fruit to eventually follow such claims of sanctification. In Palmer's eyes, the way of holiness is an eminently practical way of life that is marked by virtuous behavior and holy action. While these acts of piety do not bring about sanctification, true sanctification always results in a life of piety. This is an important point when exploring the apophatic dimension of her spirituality. It is evident from Palmer's expectations of incarnational holiness, that she does not embrace an excessive apophaticism that diminishes creation or the incarnation.

Palmer also believes that perfection (e.g. sanctification) is not an exhaustive possession of all spiritual wisdom or knowledge, but a fullness of capacity to love. In other words, the "perfected" (sanctified) Christian has the capacity to love God and neighbor wholeheartedly.[37] In this doctrine she reflects Wesley's understanding of perfection as the teleological fullness of love of God and neighbor. The fullness of love grows deeper as the sanctified believer continues to mature spiritually. There is a dynamic quality to the experience and expression of such love.

---

35. Cf. 2 Cor 2:14–16; Eph 5:1–2.

36. Palmer, *Full Salvation*, 76.

37. Palmer, *Way of Holiness*, 60–61.

Thus the lived experience of Christian sanctification is neither one devoid of human error, nor is it a static way of life that "has arrived" and does not continue to mature. These two qualifiers concerning the role of works and the presence of ongoing human frailty in sanctified believers, are necessary in order to understand what Palmer means by the second step of faith in God's promise. If one ignores Palmer's understanding of the presence of works and the presence of human frailty and simply plucks out of context her statements about naked faith in the naked Word of God, one could accuse Palmer of promoting a new kind of quietism in which experience is irrelevant to faith. When Palmer describes the second step as faith in God's promise regardless of outward signs or manifestations, she is therefore not rejecting or ignoring religious activity. Rather, she makes clear that holy activity is the outcome rather than cause of sanctification.

Palmer's reticence toward religious emotion is best understood in light of her initial struggle to experience sanctification and in her reports of ongoing severe spiritual trials in which she had to rely on "naked faith" during times of emotional despair:

> These trials, though they sometimes arose from outward causes, were generally inward and the struggle they caused is indescribable; in the midst of which she was often called to lean so entirely, "with *naked* promise," that nature was sometimes tempted in its shrinkings to say, "My God, why hast thou forsaken me?" but still holding with an unyielding grasp upon the promise, "I will never leave nor forsake thee." And believing that the Savior was treading "the wine press *alone*, and of the people there was none with him," when he gave utterance to this expression, she was checked ere she had given words to the thought, and instead of indulging in those words, which none but He who "wept that man might smile," *need* use, she said in the language of faith, "My God, thou hast not forsaken me."[38]

Palmer's apophatic mysticism is particularly evident in her approach to religious emotion and its relativization in the sanctified believer as she articulates the second step of the shorter way. Palmer has learned over the course of many years of "consolations and desolations" to accept either experience as part of the journey, while allowing neither to determine her level of commitment to God. If anything, the more

38. Palmer, *Way of Holiness*, 65–66.

desolate she feels emotionally, the more firmly she clings to the Word of God. Palmer's journey included many seasons in the dark, many bouts of emotional desolation and absence of spiritual assurance. For Palmer these seasons were experienced as a kind of testing in the wilderness, not unlike the testing of Jesus in the wilderness, whose sustenance was the naked word of God.[39] This kind of spiritual combat, as already described elsewhere, marked Palmer's spiritual journey throughout her lifetime. It is not surprising, then, that in describing the second step of the shorter way, Palmer lists emotional manifestations and emotional assurance as phenomena that may or may not accompany the initial experience of sanctification.

As is the case with religious activity, Palmer is not denying the validity or even desirability of emotional experience as part of sanctification. It seems evident from her own record of her life that she experienced many profound emotional encounters with God, and that she enjoyed deep and loving relationships with her husband, family and friends. What Palmer apparently wants to make clear is the contingency of emotional experience. She wants those who seek sanctification to know that sanctification is not a guarantee of a particular set of emotional experiences, nor should they base their testimony of God's sanctifying grace on emotional experiences. She does not want people to think they have lost sanctification because they happen to feel blue one day, or do not feel much of anything. Nor does she want people to mistakenly think that just because they are on a "high" emotionally they must be sanctified.

Palmer wants seekers to know that they can trust God's word despite shifting emotions. Her emphasis on this point has the potential to bring stability and needed rest to those who, like herself, have worn themselves out seeking a preconceived emotional experience in order to believe that God has accepted them as living sacrifices. According to Palmer, once the believer has taken genuine inventory and has offered everything on the altar of Christ, he or she may rest assured that God receives the *olah* being offered. God will sanctify the gift.

Since God promises to receive all who fully consecrate themselves to him (2 Cor 6:16—7:1), the believer has no reason to fear being rejected by God. Even if the one seeking holiness is not sure about hav-

---

39. Luke 4:1–13.

ing confessed all sin and consecrated everything to God, there is no reason to doubt because Phil 3:15 promises that if the Christian thinks incorrectly about something but is still open to God, God will surely reveal and correct the incorrect thinking.[40] The entire thrust of Old and New Testament sacrificial theology is that God longs for people to pray precisely this kind of prayer: a heartfelt prayer of entire and adoring surrender. Because of the overwhelming teaching of the Bible on God's posture toward sincere seekers, no one who prays in this way need fear that God will reject him or her.

Not only should seekers put aside fear of rejection, they should also put aside doubt, argues Palmer. To doubt that one is sanctified after having fully consecrated oneself is to doubt God's word, which is sinful according to Palmer.[41] This kind of doubt can actually prevent sanctification from taking place, since one must believe the promise of God in order to receive the promise. Along these lines Palmer stresses that one should not profess before one believes.[42]

For very scrupulous types the very temptation to doubt God's word promising sanctification may be perceived as the sin of doubting God's word, just as the temptation to lust may be perceived as the sin of lust. The distinction between being tempted to sin and actually sinning may not be distinctly perceived for many people. The degree of self-knowledge required for this step may be beyond what the average person experiences.

Telling Others

The third and final step of the shorter way is that of testimony. Indeed if this step is omitted, argues Palmer, sanctification cannot be retained. John Fletcher, one of Palmer's heroes of faith, reports that he lost the blessing of holiness five times because of failing to testify about it. Palmer begins the section of *Full Salvation* entitled "Publish It, Tell It" with Fletcher's experience, then goes on to describe the power of the Holy Spirit that came upon a camp meeting when a certain minister

---

40. Palmer, *Way of Holiness*, 137–38.

41. White, *Beauty of Holiness*, 139. For one example of Palmer's repeated emphasis on trusting and not doubting the authority of God's word see Palmer, *Full Salvation*, 47–49.

42. Palmer, *Full Salvation*, 177–79.

there finally began to testify to having been sanctified.[43] Several others present who had "lost the blessing" regained it as this man testified to the baptism of the Holy Spirit.[44] Citing Rom 10:9–10, Palmer urges those who have believed in their hearts to also "testify with their mouths" to the truth of what God has done.

Palmer follows Wesley in this step, for he also urged Christians to tell others what God has done for them.[45] Testimony is necessary because the goal of sanctification is complete love of God and neighbor, and central to the expression of that love is the sharing of what God has done. Following through to Rom 10:14, Paul writes "How, then, can they [the unsaved] call on one they have not believed in? And how can they believe in one of whom they have not heard? And how can they hear without someone preaching to them?"

The good news of the Gospel, including the news of sanctification, is to be given away, not selfishly kept as a private blessing. No experience of God is meant simply as a private gift. Everything in the believer's life is to have a larger impact upon the world. "God's gifts must be *diffused* or lost," declares Palmer. "And no one enjoying the grace but will testify to the truth of this. A light put under a bushel goes out, and then it neither enlightens ourselves nor others."[46] Testimony, like the other two steps of the shorter way, is an ongoing requirement of giving oneself away, a spiritual discipline to be practiced for the rest of one's life.

Though Palmer does not explicitly say this, there is also a psychological dimension to testifying to sanctification. Each time the sanctified believer tells others of his or her experience, the reality of his or her own sanctification is reinforced and the new paradigm of Christian life as the vow to be a living *olah* is reaffirmed.

As is the case with the first and second steps of the shorter way, the third step of testimony holds the potential for a skewed interpretation. If taken at a surface level, it could be argued that Palmer teaches magical thinking. That is, one could say she believed that all one has to do is utter the right words and regardless of heart condition or life condition, rest assured of sanctification. This criticism is unconvincing in light of the

---

43. Ibid., 60.

44. Ibid., 61–62.

45. White, *Beauty of Holiness*, 139.

46. Palmer, *Full Salvation*, 71.

corpus of Palmer's writing and the holiness of her own life. Yet this was the sharpest criticism directed against Palmer's shorter way, both in her day and now. To critics both then and now, Palmer's shorter way seemed like what Bonhoeffer called "cheap grace."[47] It seemed that Palmer was making it far too easy for sinful, spiritually fruitless believers to claim a spiritual perfection they did not possess. Here, too, a failure to understand the apophatic meaning of testimony as "naked faith" led to a misunderstanding and trivialization of Palmer's mystical theology.

Despite Palmer's repeated words about holiness of life and her warnings against Christian "professors" who failed to live as Christ in the world, despite her expositions on the meaning of "naked faith in the naked Word of God," within a short time after her death Palmer's theology underwent a significant interpretive shift. In no small part because of the theological shift, Palmerian theology moved away from its apophatic underpinnings.

What would it mean to retrieve Palmer's apophatic theology and appropriate it today, especially in Methodist contexts? How might her altar theology affect disciple formation and mission? As we shall see in the next chapter, Palmer's theology, both lived and written, place her in a unique position to serve as patron saint to Methodists who are drawn to the new monasticism.

---

47. Bonhoeffer, *Cost of Discipleship*, 45.

5

Conclusion

METHODISM IS IN SERIOUS TROUBLE IN THE UNITED STATES. IN ADdition to catastrophic losses of members throughout the past several decades, in the past twenty years the number of elders under the age of 35 has dropped from 3,219 nationwide to just 850.[1] Moreover, increasing numbers of young Methodist seminarians are ambivalent about pursuing ordination as an elder, planning instead to use their seminary education to serve bi-vocationally or in a non-itinerating position. More and more of them want to serve in non-traditional settings, or to develop and lead emerging churches and new monastic communities, situations for which their denomination is not equipped. Each week I encounter young students who are deeply conflicted over their call to ministry in light of what they experience as ossified, suffocating denominational systems. For them, the church that ought to be their greatest support has become the chief stumbling block to answering God's call. The dwindling of young elders is matched by the exodus of young adult members.

These trends in American Methodism coincide with the stunning research of David Kinnaman who set out to discover why young adults are increasingly negative toward Christianity. Kinnaman learned that among "outsiders" to Christianity who are ages 16–29, ". . . the three most common perceptions of present-day Christianity are anti-homosexual (an image held by 91 percent of young outsiders), judgmental (87 percent, and hypocritical (85 percent)."[2] In general, young adults cannot

---

1. In 1985, 15.05 percent of all United Methodist elders were under the age of 35. By 2005 the number had dropped to 4.69 percent. A Thompson, "Decline in Young Leadership Threatens Methodism's Future," 7B.

2. Kinnaman and Lyons, *Unchristian*, 27.

abide the self-serving "swagger" of Christians. They feel they must be on guard against a church that would, if given a chance, "walk all over them."[3] Kinnaman states that these perceptions of Christianity grieve young Christians who "feel disconnection between their lives today and the way Jesus lived—a mission to bring the kingdom of God into sharp focus for all people, especially those who have the deepest needs."[4]

The good news is that a new cadre of Phoebe Palmers is rising— young Methodists—with the same thirst for holiness and commitment to social justice that inspired Phoebe Palmer to defy social norms and challenge ecclesial traditions in order to answer her call. These new Methodists need a patron saint from their own tradition, a mystic and a prophet who can help them stay the course in the face of great challenge. That saint is Phoebe Palmer.

In recommending Palmer as patron saint I am not saying the new Methodists should slavishly imitate everything she said and did. She was, after all, quite human. What is to be desired, rather, is for her "mantle" to fall upon the new Methodists, her fire and commitment and insistence upon the way of holiness. There are several ways in which Palmer is the patron saint for the new Methodists. Indeed, Palmer shows us from her nineteenth century social context how twenty-first century Methodists can and should embrace the new monasticism as a deeply Wesleyan form of Christian life.[5] For the new monasticism is nothing less than a new holiness movement.

Like the "old" monasticism, new monasticism is a grassroots, prophetic renewal movement that is calling the church back to its missional vocation. Communities are diverse in every possible way: theologically, geographically, and in terms of how members live their Christian commitments. Shane Claiborne's Simple Way community in Philadelphia is one model that is, as its name indicates, simple. Simple Way evolved out of events in which Claiborne and his friends began to sneak out of their college dorms at night to spend time with homeless people.[6] Soon they were involved in protesting a denomination that had asked the city to evict homeless people from one of its abandoned church build-

---

3. Ibid., 26.

4. Ibid., 35.

5. For a list of the twelve marks and a variety of articles and links on the ecumenical new monastic movement see www.newmonasticism.org.

6. Claiborne, *Irresistible Revolution*, 47–51. Also see Bessenecker, *The New Friars*.

ings. The story of Simple Way, *The Irresistible Revolution*, has influenced many Christians to move toward a new monastic way of life. Jim Wallis describes the book as the "manifesto for a new generation."[7]

There are other forms of new monastic communities, some of them urban, some rural. In all of them there is a common theme, the desire to live the gospel with greater integrity. According to Jonathan Wilson-Hartgrove and others within the network of new monastic communities, there are twelve marks that are common to the new monasticism:

1. Relocation to abandoned places of the empire
2. Sharing economic resources with fellow community members
3. Hospitality to the stranger
4. Lament for racial divisions within the church and our communities
5. Humble submission to Christ's body, the church
6. Intentional formation in the way of Christ and the rule of the community along the lines of the old novitiate
7. Nurturing common life among members of intentional community
8. Support for celibate singles alongside monogamous married couples and their children
9. Geographical proximity to community members who share a common rule of life
10. Care for the plot of God's earth given to us along with support of our local economies
11. Peacemaking in the midst of violence and conflict resolution along the lines of Matthew 18
12. Commitment to a disciplined contemplative life[8]

Patron saints gain such standing because of their lives and their teaching. To better understand Palmer's importance as a spiritual guide for the new Methodists today, let us think first about her Shorter Way, including her Altar Theology, then reflect upon the practices of her own

---

7. Ibid., 11.

8. Rutba House, *Schools for Conversion*, Jonathan Wilson-Hartgrove tells the story of the inspiration for the naming of Rutba House, the new monastic community he and his wife Leah founded in Durham, NC, in *To Baghdad and Beyond*.

"monastic" rule, steeped as they were in Wesleyan theology and emerging from her mystical spirituality.

For Palmer, sanctification is the way of holiness made possible by three elements of human response to God that are both episodic and a continuous process. These are consecration, naked faith, and testimony.

Palmer clearly believed that consecration is an ongoing process, an intentional placing of oneself and all that one has on the altar of Jesus. The altar, Jesus, makes the gift holy. We can think of this aspect of the Shorter Way as ordering one's life around prayer, or to use the language of monasticism, following a rule of life. In particular, the atmosphere of prayer in this rule of life is one of surrender to God and God's missional purposes in the world. It is a posture of relinquishment (the *via negativa*) of all that one has and all that one is, as a living sacrifice. Paradoxically this life of kenotic prayer becomes a life of healing and integration as one includes in the gifts placed on the altar, one's brokenness, grief, failures, sins, and mistakes. These too, are made holy by Jesus, to become a source of life and good news for others. As Richard Rohr explains so beautifully, in this life of consecration we come to understand that in the mystery of God's redemption, everything about our lives "belongs."[9] Thus the rule of life under the rubric of "consecration" leads one home to oneself and God, as nothing else can. This homecoming is what makes genuine community possible. And for the new monasticism, community is the core of missional life.

The second element of Palmer's Shorter Way is naked faith, the belief that God is faithful and true to God's word regardless of shifting human emotions and changing circumstances. It is devotion to the God who is love even through a dark night of the soul. Naked faith means living, speaking and praying the truth of God's love even when God seems to have disappeared, the ultimate form of apophatic mysticism.

No one in the twentieth century embodied the love of Jesus more than Mother Teresa, founder of the Missionaries of Charity. When Mother Teresa's private writings and theological reflections were published in 2007,[10] many readers were shocked and disturbed to learn that the beloved sister spent much of her adult life in a dark night of the

9. Rohr, *Everything Belongs*, 20–21.
10. Mother Teresa, *Come Be My Light*.

soul, unable to feel the presence of God except as mediated through the suffering people of Calcutta.

Mother Teresa embodied the fidelity of Palmer's second step of naked faith. As was the case with Palmer, Mother Teresa experienced great anguish of soul and internal conflicts, as well as struggles with church officials as she continued to faithfully live her call. Yet she persevered, in naked faith. Mother Teresa is a primary source of inspiration for Shane Claiborne and many other new monastic Christians.

Living with naked faith in the naked word of God is neither fideistic sentimentality, nor an uncritical hermeneutic of scripture. It is the unfathomable spiritual depth of Palmer, a young woman who turns the grief over the death of her children into loving service to thousands. Naked faith is the commitment of Christians to say yes to God's call to mission, even though it means sacrifice: pastoring bi-vocationally so that one can serve among the urban and rural poor, choosing to plant a new congregation in the inner city rather than a booming suburb. It means saying yes to God's call even though one's denomination has no systems to contain new monastic communities or to ordain those who are called to unpaid service in such communities. It means creating new paradigms of ministry to reach people the church has turned away. This kind of naked faith is at the heart of the new monasticism.

The third element of the Shorter Way is testimony, telling others what God has done. This telling is not only verbal proclamation, but a holistic outreach that brings healing and life to individuals and communities. It is a lifestyle that brings about transformation. Palmer declared repeatedly that unless one testified to what God has done, one would lose the blessing. Much of the reason the "glory has left the temple" of American Methodism is that it is not living in a holistic way, the gospel that it proclaims. Methodism has all but lost "the blessing." But the new monastics believe that there is hope, and that the new monasticism needs to remain anchored in the historic, established church.[11] The church can regain its missional vocation with the loving and humble presence of the new monasticism, and the new monasticism can be protected from becoming ingrown, legalistic and oppressive by remaining grounded in the "great traditions" of the church.[12] Each can see the other as a divine,

11. This is the subject of Jonathan Wilson-Hartgrove's *New Monasticism*.

12. Kauffman, "Mark 5," 68–75.

life-giving gift. The retrieval of Palmer as Methodism's own mystic and saint can help Methodism to affirm and support the new Methodists. Conversely, Palmer's anti-schismatic stance toward her own tradition can help the new Methodists remain grounded in the great tradition.

As we have seen in this brief overview, a Palmerian theology of holiness for today is in many ways exemplary for the new Methodists who hunger for a new monastic ecclesiology. Palmer's life also models for the church today, what the way of holiness looks like. Palmer herself is an exemplar for the new Methodists in the following ways, many of which coincide with the Twelve Marks of the New Monasticism.

First, Palmer followed a disciplined rule of life, as outlined in chapter 1. "Closet duties," or regular prayer through the day, ordered the rest of her life and were the source of her missional power. Next, Palmer practiced spiritual life with fellow sojourners through the Tuesday meetings for the promotion of Holiness. These gatherings became the locus of transformation for many people, including clergy, bishops and theologians. The replication of Tuesday meetings by Palmer's disciples was one of the outcomes of this practice, bearing many parallels to Catholic reformers whose followers went on to establish networks of communities, such as the Franciscans.

Palmer's way of holiness had strong components of social justice, evident in her helping to found Five Points Mission, and in numerous other justice ministries with which she was engaged. As a powerful and outspoken advocate for the right of women to engage in public ministry, Palmer became a catalyst for the transformation of many women who went on to establish greater civil rights for women, including Francis Willard. Palmer's life of kenosis expressed itself in these and many other ways.

Unlike many Christians today who believe that holiness requires women to "focus on the family," Palmer believed that too narrow a view of family hindered the work of God and was contrary to the gospel. Thus while she loved her husband and children, she intentionally placed them "on the altar" so that she could love God's family with greater fidelity.

In the face of her public ministry, her criticism of the church as it silenced women and ignored the way of holiness, Palmer received much criticism in her lifetime. Yet she persevered. Like Mother Teresa, Palmer counted success as a matter of faithfulness to God, something that might not be measurable in terms of numbers and money.

As we have seen, Palmer was an extraordinary Christian mystic, one whose life and thought were prophetic, healing, and liberating for those who had "ears to hear." In many ways Palmer's light was put under a bushel by her own Methodist tradition so that her gifts were all but lost. The celebration of Palmer's stature as one of the great mystics of the church and as the premier apophatic mystic of Methodism, holds many fruitful possibilities for changing the landscape of Methodist studies. Palmer can help Methodism mature into a fuller, more ecumenically connected spirituality that honors and embraces apophatic mysticism. Moreover, with Palmer as the patron saint for the new Methodists, the Mother of the holiness movement could once again lead Methodists into a powerful new day.

Bibliography

Writings of Phoebe Palmer

Palmer, Phoebe. "The Cleansing Wave." Phoebe W. Palmer, "The Cleansing Wave." Online: http://www.cyberhymnal.org/htm/c/l/cleansin.htm.

———. *Entire Devotion to God*. 14th ed. New York: n.p., 1853; reprint ed., Salem, OH: Schmul, 1979.

———. *Faith and Its Effects: Or Fragments from My Portfolio*. New York: Phoebe Palmer, 1854. Reprint ed., *The Devotional Writing of Phoebe Palmer*. The Higher Christian Life Series. New York: Garland, 1986.

———. *Incidental Illustrations of the Economy of Salvation, Its Doctrines and Duties*. Toronto: G. R. Sanderson, 1855. Selections republished as *Full Salvation: Its Doctrine and Duties*. Salem, OH: Schmul, n.d.

———. *The Promise of the Father*. New York: Palmer, 1859. Salem, OH: Schmul, n.d.

———. *Selected Writings*. Edited by Thomas C. Oden. Sources of American Spirituality Series. New York: Paulist, 1988.

———. *The Way of Holiness, with Notes by the Way*. New York: Piercy and Reed, 1843. New York: Palmer and Hughes, 1867. Salem, OH: Schmul, n.d.

Other Works Consulted

"Apostolic Christian Church: Lifestyle." Online: http://www.apostolicchristian.org/.

Armstrong, Chris R. "Ravished Heart or Naked Faith: The Kernel and Husk of Phoebe Palmer." Presented at the Society for Pentecostal Studies, Cleveland, TN, March 13, 1998.

Attridge, Harold W. *The Epistle to the Hebrews*. Hermeneia Commentary Series. Philadelphia, PA: Fortress, 1989.

Averbeck, Richard. "Olah." In *New International Dictionary of OT Theology and Exegesis*, 405–15. Grand Rapids, MI: Zondervan, 1997.

Balthasar, Hans Urs von. *Prayer*. Translated by Graham Harrison. San Francisco, CA: Ignatius, 1986.

Bassett, Paul Merritt. "The Theological Identity of the North American Holiness Movement." In *The Variety of American Evangelicalism*, edited by Donald W. Dayton and Robert K. Johnston. Knoxville: The University of Tennessee Press, 1991.

Bautz, Friedrich Wilhelm. "Robert d'Andilly Arnauld." *Kirchenlexicon*. Online: http://www.bautz.de/bbkl/a/arnauld_r.shtml.

Beasley-Topliffe, Keith, editor. *A Longing for Holiness: Selected Writings of John Wesley*. Nashville, TN: Upper Room, 1997.

Bessenecker, Scott A. *The New Friars*. Downer's Grove, IL: InterVarsity, 2006.

Bonhoeffer, Dietrich. *The Cost of Discipleship*. New York: Macmillan, 1963.

Brown, Francis, S. R. Driver, and Charles A. Briggs. *The New Brown, Driver, Briggs, Gesenius Hebrew and English Lexicon*. Peabody, MA: Hendrickson, 1979.

Brown, Kenneth O. *A History of Camp Sychar*. Hazelton, PA: Holiness Archives, 2000.

———. *Indian Springs Holiness Camp Meeting: A History of the "Greatest Camp Meeting in the South."* Hazelton, PA: Holiness Archives, 2000.

———. *Inskip, McDonald, Fowler: "Wholly and Forever Thine"*. Hazelton, PA: Holiness Archives, 1999.

Bruce, F. F. *The Epistle to the Hebrews*. Grand Rapids, MI: Eerdmans, 1990.

Bruyneel, Sally. "Phoebe Palmer, Mother of the Holiness Movement." *Priscilla Papers* 12.2 (1998) 1–2.

Bundy, David. "Visions of Sanctification: Themes of Orthodoxy in the Methodist, Holiness, and Pentecostal Traditions." *Wesleyan Theological Journal* 39 (2004) 104–36.

Carr, Sara "Brownsville Revival." Online: http://religiousmovements.lib.virginia.edu/nrms/Brownsv.html.

Carvosso, William. *A Memoir of Mr. William Carvosso*. New York: Carlton & Phillips, 1853.

Christensen, Michael J. "Theosis and Sanctification: John Wesley's Reformulation of a Patristic Doctrine." *Wesleyan Theological Journal* 31 (1996) 71–93.

Claiborne, Shane. *The Irresistible Revolution*. Grand Rapids, MI: Zondervan, 2006.

Coffing, Karen B. "Character and Personality: Phoebe Palmer and Aimee Semple McPherson as Mirrors of American Culture." *Fides et Historia* 28 (1996) 48–67.

Dayton, Donald. *Theological Roots of Pentecostalism*. Grand Rapids, MI: Asbury, 1987.

DeVries, George, Jr. "Phoebe Palmer and Spiritual Independence." *The Reformed Journal* 37 (1987) 3–5.

Dieter, Melvin Easterday. "The Development of Nineteenth Century Holiness Theology." *Wesleyan Theological Journal* 20.1 (1985) 61–77.

———. *The Holiness Revival of the Nineteenth Century*. Metuchen, NJ: Scarecrow, 1980.

Dieter, Melvin, editor. *The 19th Century Holiness Movement*. Vol. 4, Great Holiness Classics Series. Kansas City, MO: Beacon Hill, 1998.

Drury, Keith. "The Holiness Movement: Dead or Alive?" Online: http://www.cresourcei.org/hmovement.html.

Dupré, Louis. *The Deeper Life: An Introduction to Christian Mysticism*. New York: Crossroad, 1981.

Eckhart, Meister. *Meister Eckhart*. Translated by Raymond B. Blakney. New York: Harper Torchbooks, 1941.

Egan, Harvey D. "Christian Apophatic and Kataphatic Mysticisms." *Theological Studies* 39 (1978) 399–426.

———. *Christian Mysticism: the Future of a Tradition*. New York: Pueblo, 1984.

Egan, Keith. "Thérèse of Lisieux." In *New Dictionary of Catholic Spirituality*, 123. Collegeville, MN: Liturgical, 1993.

Fitzmier, J. R. "Second Great Awakening." In *Dictionary of Christianity in America*, 1067–68. Downer's Grove, IL: Intervarsity, 1990.

Flannery, Austin, editor. *Vatican Council II*. Revised edition. Northport, NY: Costello, 1996.

Fletcher, John. *Beauties of Fletcher: Being Extracts from His Checks to Antinomianism in a Series of Letters to Rev. Mr. Shirley and Mr. Hill*. Edited by T. Spicer. New York: Lane & Sandford, 1843.

———. *Christian Perfection: Being an Extract from the Rev. John Fletcher's Treatise on That Subject*. New York: Carlton & Porter, n.d.

———. *The Works of John Fletcher*. Vols. 1–4. New York: Waugh and Mason, 1835.

Freemantle, Anne, editor. *The Protestant Mystics*. With an Introduction by W.H. Auden. New York: Mentor, 1964.

Galea, Kate P. Crawford. "Anchored Behind the Veil: Mystical Vision as a Possible Source of Authority in the Ministry of Phoebe Palmer." *Methodist History* 31 (1993) 236–47.

Grider, J. Kenneth. *Entire Sanctification: the Distinctive Doctrine of Wesleyanism*. Kansas City, MO: Beacon Hill, 1980.

Harkness, Georgia. *Mysticism: Its Meaning and Message*. Nashville: Abingdon, 1973.

Hassey, Janette. *No Time for Silence: Evangelical Women in Public Ministry Around the Turn of the Century*. Grand Rapids, MI: Zondervan, 1986.

Heath, Elaine A. "The *Via Negativa* in the Life and Writing of Phoebe Palmer." *Wesleyan Theological Journal* 41 (2006) 87–111.

Heidinger, James V. II. "Publisher's Welcome." *Good News Home Page*. Online: http://www.goodnewsmag.org/, 2002.

Hoffman, Elisha A. "Is Your All on the Altar?" Online: http://www.cyberhymnal.org/htm/i/s/isyoural.htm, 1900.

Howard, Ivan. "Wesley Versus Phoebe Palmer: An Extended Controversy." *Wesleyan Theological Journal* 6 (1971) 31–40.

Hovet, Theodore. "Phoebe Palmer's Altar Phraseology and the Spiritual Dimension of Woman's Sphere." *Journal of Religion* 63 (1983) 264–80.

Hügel, Friedrich von. *The Mystical Element of Religion as Studied in Saint Catherine of Genoa and Her Friends*. 2 Vols., 2nd ed. London: Dent, 1923.

Hughes, George. *Fragrant Memories of the Tuesday Meeting and the Guide to Holiness and Their Fifty Years' Work for Jesus*. New York: Palmer and Hughes, 1886; Salem, OH: Schmul, 1988.

Imbach, Jeffrey. *The Recovery of Love: Christian Mysticism and the Addictive Society*. With a Foreword by Henri J.M. Nouwen. New York: Crossroad, 1992.

Irons, Kendra Weddle. "Phoebe Palmer: Chosen, Tried, Triumphant; An Examination of Her Calling in Light of Current Research." *Methodist History* 37 (1998) 28–36.

Jantzen, Grace M. *Power, Gender and Christian Mysticism*. Cambridge: Cambridge University Press, 1995.

Jeffrey, David Lyle, editor. *A Burning and Shining Light: English Spirituality in the Age of Wesley*. Grand Rapids, MI: Eerdmans, 1987.

John of the Cross. *The Dark Night of the Soul*. Edited and translated by E. Allison Peers. Online: http://www.ccel.org/j/john_cross/dark_night/dark_night.html.

Johnston, William. *Arise, My Love: Mysticism for a New Era*. Maryknoll: Orbis, 2000.

————, editor. *The Cloud of Unknowing and The Book of Privy Counseling*. New York, NY: Image, Doubleday, 1973.

————. *Mystical Theology*. San Francisco: HarperCollins, 1995.

Jones, Charles Edwin. *A Guide to the Study of the Holiness Movement*. Metuchen, NJ: Scarecrow, and the American Theological Library Association, 1974.

————. "The Inverted Shadow of Phoebe Palmer." *Wesleyan Theological Journal* 31 (1996) 120–31.

————. *Perfectionist Persuasion: The Holiness Movement and American Methodism, 1867–1936*. Metuchen, NJ: Scarecrow, 1974.

————. "The Posthumous Pilgrimage of Phoebe Palmer." *Methodist History* 35 (1997) 203–13.

Jones, Cheslyn, Geoffrey Wainwright, and Edward Yarnold, editors. *The Study of Spirituality*. New York: Oxford University Press, 1986.

Julian of Norwich. *Showings*. Classics of Western Spirituality Series. Translated and with an Introduction by Edmund Colledge and James Walsh. New York: Paulist, 1978.

Keller, Rosemary Skinner, editor. *Spirituality and Social Responsibility: Vocational Vision of Women in the United Methodist Tradition*. Nashville, TN: Abingdon, 1993.

Kelsey, Morton. *Dreams: A Way to Listen to God*. New York: Paulist. 1978.

————. *Encounter with God*. London: Hodder and Stoughton, 1974.

————. *Psychology, Medicine and Christian Healing*. San Francisco, CA: Harper-SanFrancisco, 1988.

Kierkegaard, Soren. *Purity of Heart Is to Will One Thing*. Translated by Douglas V. Steere. New York: Harper, 1938.

Kinnaman, David and Gabe Lyons. *Unchristian: What a New Generation Really Thinks about Christianity . . . and Why It Matters*. Grand Rapids, MI: Baker, 2008.

LaCugna, Catherine Mowry. *God For Us: The Trinity and Christian Life*. San Francisco, CA: Harper Collins, 1993.

Lancaster, John. *The Life of Lady Maxwell*. New York: Mason and Lane, 1837.

Lane, William L. *Hebrews 9–13*. Vol. 48 of *Word Biblical Commentary*. Dallas, TX: Word, 1991.

Langford, Thomas A. *Practical Divinity: Theology in the Wesleyan Tradition*. Nashville, TN: Abingdon, 1983.

Leclerc, Diane. "Gendered Sin? Gendered Holiness? Historical Considerations, Homiletical Implications." *Wesleyan Theological Journal* 39 (2004) 54–73.

————. *Singleness of Heart: Gender, Sin and Holiness in Historical Perspective*. Lanham, MD: Scarecrow, 2001.

————. "Wesleyan Holiness Feminist Hermeneutics: Historical Rendering, Current Considerations." *Wesleyan Theological Journal* 36 (2001) 105–32.

————. "A Woman's Way of Holiness: An Analysis of Phoebe Palmer's Theology with Reflection on its Intrinsic Feminist Implications." *American Society of Church History Papers*. Lisle, IL: 160th Annual Conference of the American Society of Church History, April 11–13, 1996; Portland, OR: Theological Research Exchange Network, 1996.

Livingstone, Elizabeth A., editor. *The Concise Oxford Dictionary of the Christian Church*. New York: Oxford University Press, 1990.

Lossky, Vladimir. *The Mystical Theology of the Eastern Church*. Translated by members of the Fellowship of St. Aban and St. Sergius. Old Woking, Surrey: Unwin, 1957.

Louth, Andrew. *The Origins of the Christian Mystical Tradition from Plato to Denys*. Oxford: Oxford University Press, 1981.

Lowery, Kevin T. "A Fork in the Wesleyan Road: Phoebe Palmer and the Appropriation of Christian Perfection." *Wesleyan Theological Journal* 36 (2001) 187–222.

Maddox, Randy L. *Responsible Grace: John Wesley's Practical Theology*. Nashville, TN: Kingswood, 1994.

Mallory, Marilyn May. *Christian Mysticism Transcending Techniques*. Amsterdam: Van Gorcum Assen, 1977.

Manual. Online: http://www.bible.ca/cr-Nazarene.htm.

McBrien, Richard P., editor. *The HarperCollins Encyclopedia of Catholicism*. San Francisco, CA: HarperCollins, 1995.

McFadden, Maragaret. "The Ironies of Pentecost: Phoebe Palmer, World Evangelism and Female Networks." *Methodist History* 31.2 (1993) 63–75.

McGinn, Bernard. *The Presence of God*. Vol. 1, *The Foundations of Mysticism*. New York: Crossroad, 1992.

———. "Quo Vadis? Reflections on the Current Study of Mysticism." *Christian Spirituality Bulletin* 6 (1998) 13–21.

McGonigle, Thomas D. "Three Ways." In *The New Dictionary of Catholic Spirituality*, edited by Michael Downey, 963–65. Collegeville, MN: Liturgical, 1993.

———. "Union, Unitive Way." In *The New Dictionary of Catholic Spirituality*, edited by Michael Downey, 987–88. Collegeville, MN: Liturgical, 1993.

McIntosh, Mark A. *Mystical Theology*. Oxford: Blackwell, 1998.

Mother Teresa. *Come Be My Light*. Edited by Brian Kolodiejchuk. New York: Doubleday, 2007.

Nemeck, Francis Kelly, and Marie Theresa Coombs. *O Blessed Night*. New York: Alba, 1991.

———. *The Spiritual Journey*. Collegeville, MN: Liturgical, 1987.

Norwood, Frederick A. *The Story of American Methodism*. Nashville, TN: Abingdon, 1974.

Nouwen, Henri J. M. *Reaching Out*. Garden City, NY: Doubleday, 1975.

Oden, Thomas C. *John Wesley's Scriptural Christianity: A Plain Exposition of His Teaching on Christian Doctrine*. Grand Rapids, MI: Zondervan, 1994.

———, editor. *Selected Writings of Phoebe Palmer*. Sources of American Spirituality Series. New York: Paulist, 1988.

"Official Website for Promise Keepers." Online: http://www.promisekeepers.org/.

Orcibal, Jean. "The Theological Originality of John Wesley and Continental Spirituality." In *A History of the Methodist Church in Great Britain*, edited by Rupert Davies and Gordon Rupp, 1:81–112. London: Epworth, 1965.

Ouspensky, Leonid, and Vladimir Lossky. *The Meaning of Icons*. Crestwood, NY: St. Vladimir's Seminary Press, 1989.

Outler, Albert C. *Evangelism and Theology in a Wesleyan Spirit*. Nashville, TN: Discipleship, 1996.

Pannikar, Raimon. *Invisible Harmony: Essays on Contemplation and Responsibility*. Edited by Harry James Cargas. Minneapolis, MN: Fortress, 1995.

Peck, M. Scott. *People of the Lie*. New York: Touchstone, 1983.

Pennington, M. Basil, Alan Jones, and Mark Booth. *The Living Testament*. San Francisco, CA: Harper & Row, 1985.

Peters, Ted. *Sin: Radical Evil in Soul and Society*. Grand Rapids, MI: Eerdmans, 1994.

Portersfield, Amanda. "Phoebe Palmer." In *Women in New Worlds Conference Papers*. Madison, NJ: United Methodist Church Archives, General Commission on Archives and History, 1980.

Railton, George Scott. *Madame Jeanne de la Mothe Guyon: Educated in the Convents, Saved at the Foot of the Cross*. New York: The Salvation Army, 1885.

Rakestraw, Robert V. "Becoming like God: an Evangelical Doctrine of Theosis." *Journal of Evangelical Theological Society* 40 (1997) 257–69.

Raser, Harold E. *Phoebe Palmer: Her Life and Thought*. Lewiston, NY: Mellen, 1987.

Reid, Daniel G., Robert D. Linder, et al., editors. *Dictionary of Christianity in America*. Downers Grove: InterVarsity, 1990.

Roberts, Bernadette. *The Experience of No Self*. Boston, MA: Shambala, 1984.

Rogers, Hester Ann. *An Account of the Experience of Hester Ann Rogers and Her Funeral Sermon*. New York: Carlton & Phillips, 1853.

Rohr, Richard. *Everything Belongs*. New York: Crossroad, 1999.

Rutba House, editor. *Schools for Conversion: 12 Marks of a New Monasticism*. Eugene, OR: Cascade, 2005.

Sahadat, John. "The Interreligious Study of Mysticism and a Sense of Universality." *Journal of Ecumenical Studies* 22 (1985) 292–311.

Salter, Darius. "Mysticism in American Wesleyanism: Thomas Upham." *Wesleyan Theological Journal* 20 (1985) 94–107.

Schneiders, Sandra M. "The Study of Christian Spirituality: Contours and Dynamics of a Discipline." *Christian Spirituality Bulletin* 6 (1998) 1, 3–12.

Schwarz, Hans. *Evil: A Historical and Theological Perspective*. Minneapolis, MN: Fortress, 1995.

Schweitzer, Franz-Josef. "Von Marguerite von Porete (d1310) bis Mme. Guyon (d1717) Frauenmystik im Konflikt mit der Kirche." In *Frauenmystik im Mittelalter*. Ostfildern bei Stuttgart: Schwabenverlag, 1985.

Simmons, Dale. "Phoebe Palmer—Enjoli Woman or Enigma? A Review of the Recent Scholarship on Phoebe Palmer." *Wesleyan/Holiness Studies Center Bulletin* 30 (1996) 1, 4.

Smith, Timothy. "John Wesley's Religion in Thomas Jefferson's America." In *The 19th Century Holiness movement*, edited by Melvin Dieter. Kansas City, MO: Beacon Hill, 1998.

Spencer, Aída Besançon. *Beyond the Curse*. Nashville, TN: Thomas Nelson, 1985.

Sweet, William Warren. *Methodism in American History*. Revised edition. Nashville, TN: Abingdon, 1954.

St. John of the Cross. *The Dark Night of the Soul*. Edited by E. Allison Peers. http://www.ccel.org/j/john_cross/dark_night/dark_night.html.

St. Teresa of Avila. *Collected Works: The Book of Her Life, Spiritual Testimonies, Soliloquies*. Translated by Kieran Kavanaugh and Otilio Rodriguez. Washington DC: ICS, 1976.

———, "*De Quatuor Gradibus Violentae Charitatis*." In *Patrologia Latina*, edited by Jacques-Paul Migne. Alexandria, VA : Chadwyck-Healey, 1995. vol. cxcvi.

St. Thérèse of Lisieux. *Story of a Soul*. 3rd ed. Translated by John Clarke. Washington DC: ICS, 1996.

Taves, Ann. *Fits, Trances and Visions: Experiencing Religion and Explaining Experience from Wesley to James*. Princeton, NY: Princeton University Press, 1999.

Thompson, Andrew C. "Decline in Young Leadership Threatens Methodism's Future." *United Methodist Reporter* 152.52 (2006) 7B.

Thompson, William M. *Christology and Spirituality*. New York: Crossroad, 1991.

———. *Fire and Light: the Saints and Theology*. New York: Paulist, 1987.

———. *The Struggle for Theology's Soul*. New York: Crossroad, 1996.

Toon, Peter. *Spiritual Companions: An Introduction to the Christian Classics*. Grand Rapids, MI: Baker, 1990.

Tracy, David. *Plurality and Ambiguity*. Chicago, IL: University of Chicago Press, 1994.

Truesdale, Al. "Reification of the Experience of Entire Sanctification in the American Holiness Movement." *Wesleyan Theological Journal* 30 (1996) 95–119.

Tucker, Ruth A. and Walter Liefeld. *Daughters of the Church*. Grand Rapids, MI: Zondervan, 1987.

Turner, Denys. *The Darkness of God: Negativity in Christian Mysticism*. Cambridge: Cambridge University Press, 1995.

Tuttle, Robert G. *Mysticism in the Wesleyan Tradition*. Grand Rapids, MI: Francis Asbury Press, 1989.

Underhill, Evelyn. *Mysticism*. New York: Meridian, 1955.

———. *Practical Mysticism*. New York: Dutton, 1915. 1943.

Wainwright, Geoffrey. *Doxology*. New York: Oxford University Press, 1980.

Wall, Ernest. "I Commend Unto You Phoebe." *Religion in Life* 26 (1957) 396–408.

Ward, Patricia A. "Madame Guyon and Experiential Theology in America." *Church History* 67 (1998) 485–98.

Ware, Steven L. "Phoebe Palmer and the Male Leaders of the Holiness Renewal." *American Society of Church History Papers*. Lisle, IL: 160th Annual Conference of the American Society of Church History, April 11–13, 1996; Portland, OR: Theological Research Exchange Network, 1996.

Watson, David Lowes. *The Early Methodist Class Meeting: Its Origins and Significance*. Nashville, TN: Discipleship, 1991.

Wenham, Gordon J. *The Book of Leviticus*. The New International Commentary on the Old Testament Series. Grand Rapids, MI: Eerdmans, 1979.

Wesley, John. *John Wesley's Journal*. Abridged by Nehemiah Curnock. New York: Philosophical Library, 1951.

Wheatley, Richard. *The Life and Letters of Mrs. Phoebe Palmer*. New York: Palmer, 1881; New York: Garland, 1984.

Whidden, Woodrow. "Eschatology, Soteriology, and Social Activism in Four Mid-Nineteenth Century Holiness Methodists." *Wesleyan Theological Journal* 29 (1994) 92–110.

White, Charles Edward. *The Beauty of Holiness: Phoebe Palmer as Theologian, Revivalist, Feminist and Humanitarian*. Grand Rapids, MI: Asbury, 1986.

———. "Phoebe Palmer and the Development of Pentecostal Pneumatology." *Wesleyan Theological Journal* 23 (1988) 198–212.

————. "What the Holy Spirit Can and Cannot Do: the Ambiguities of Phoebe Palmer's Theology of Experience." *Wesleyan Theological Journal* 20 (1985) 108–21.

Whitney, Barry L. *What Are They Saying About God and Evil?* New York: Paulist, 1989.

Willimon, William, and Robert Wilson. *Rekindling the Flame.* Nashville, TN: Abingdon, 1987.

Wilson-Hartgrove, Jonathan. *New Monasticism: What It Has to Say to Today's Church.* Grand Rapids, MI: Brazos, 2008.

————. *To Baghdad and Beyond: How I Got Born Again in Babylon.* Eugene, OR: Cascade, 2005.